notebook notions

notebook notions

Using a writer's notebook to harvest ideas and transform your teaching

ALAN J WRIGHT

Published in 2026 by Amba Press, Melbourne, Australia
www.ambapress.com.au

© Alan j Wright 2026

All rights reserved. No part of this book may be reproduced or transmitted in any form or by any means, electronic or mechanical, including photocopying, recording or by any information storage and retrieval system, without prior permission in writing from the publisher.

Cover design: Tess McCabe
Internal design: Amba Press
Editor: Andrew Campbell

ISBN: 9781923403420 (pbk)
ISBN: 9781923403437 (ebk)

A catalogue record for this book is available from the National Library of Australia.

For all those unwitting collaborators
whose words lifted me up.

Risky Words

I sit at my desk some mornings
Confronted by slips of paper
Scribbled lists
And a head full of loosely connected thoughts
Fragments of a dream perhaps
I link them tenuously in my morning mind
Sorting them
Before writing…
I must remain courageous
I must a risk taker be
And write to the edges of thought and idea
Remembering always
The best writing
Requires such daring
Memories like ghosts float by
Lingering for just enough time
To ignite in my head
I recall. I record
And words spill across the pages of my humble notebook
I am living life twice
Scribing questionable versions of reclaimed truths
My voice. My choice.

Alan j Wright

PREFACE

Many teachers do not possess a vision of themselves as writers. The origin of this disconnect can frequently be traced back to their own school experiences with writing and the way it was presented. In many instances their writing history involved tightly controlled assignments where a teacher made all the decisions concerning topic, genre and sometimes the word limit, the notion of writing independently seldom a classroom consideration.

The young writer's competency may have been determined by a teacher's brief, sometimes harsh written remarks or a rather subjective mark out of ten or a letter grade, with such judgments scratched across the written piece in red ink that made the page look like a crime scene.

The accumulation of such dispiriting writing experiences frequently leads to a conscious uncoupling from the act of writing for pleasure, because pleasure was never associated with that initial experience. Aversion to writing is the sad outcome.

In my own case, I came through my early education with these same restrictive approaches to writing in place. However, I was fortunate that within me was a compelling urge to forge a relationship with pen, paper and words, and this became my rock. I entered teaching as a teacher who wrote. Across my career I have become a writer who teaches.

Writing in fact makes us better teachers. It helps us appreciate the joys and struggles confronting the young, inexperienced writers with whom we work. It brings energy to the classroom. We are endowed with a responsibility to share the talents and knowledge acquired from our literate lives. Bringing writing and the stories connected with it offers an exciting prospect. I am reminded of the powerful words of Annie Dillard (1990) in her book *The Writing Life*:

> ... the impulse to keep to yourself what you have learned is not only shameful, it is destructive. Anything you do not give freely and abundantly becomes lost to you. You open your safe and find ashes.

Dillard's words are unequivocal. Writing alongside inexperienced writers is too good an opportunity to let slip or ignore. Your writing possesses the potential to provide insight and give confidence to young writers. Your writing actions can give hope and inspiration to your fellow educators.

When a teacher chooses to write, it allows less experienced, highly impressionable writers to see firsthand the process of writing – from the spark of an idea through to the organisation of the text, through the struggle and problem-solving to the eventual sharing of words with an audience. It is a demonstration of powerful creative actions. It is the sharing of a lifelong gift.

In this book I am sharing lessons and understandings acquired as a teacher and writer across a rewarding career in education. Its foundation is built on personal and professional considerations arising from a conscious decision to be a teacher who writes. My notebook life has contributed immeasurably to my writing pleasure. It has provided the launching pad for all my writing projects across my career. These notebooks represent the footprints of my life. As the inspiring writing of Donald Graves (1983) reminded me, the words are proof of my existence.

In its simplest form, the notebook is a writer's resource, a risk-free place to collect potential ideas, explore and experiment. I have used it continuously to inform my teaching of writing. It is a trusted reference point.

While there is more than one way to structure a writer's notebook, I am presenting the actions that have worked for me for many years. I am sharing some of the accumulated insights gained from this long and satisfying writing journey. Notebooks are as unique as the writers who write in them. I want to support you to step out on your own journey.

As the most proficient writer in your classroom, you should feel confident in giving your writing a leading role in the important work of growing young readers and writers. It is an opportunity to develop within them a genuine sense of their own agency as writers.

I hope you come away with renewed understanding of how the writer's notebook can support your teaching and writing efforts. I hope my words deliver a sense of renewed energy for writing. If we want our inexperienced student writers to be risk-takers, it is imperative we lead the way …

Alan j Wright

ACKNOWLEDGEMENTS

This book is about a writing journey and the people and events that have helped nourish and sustain it. It is about all those student writers I have written for and with. It is about teachers who trusted me sufficiently to take up their pens and join me as teachers who write.

Writing is often a solitary pursuit; the writer disappears for a time in order to return with something to share with a reader. That requires tolerance and understanding on the part of those close to the writer. My wife, esteemed educator Vicki Froomes, epitomises that quality by supporting my passion for writing. I remain ever grateful for that critical support and fearless analysis. She has lived through all the twists and turns of this long journey. She has stuck with me even when I was living deep inside my writer's mind.

My late uncle, the Reverend John William Henry Smith, theologian and fellow writer, was always a valued sounding board for writing and its challenges and rewards. John was a lifelong mentor. Among other things, he taught me the value of being quietly subversive.

My great friend and colleague Barry Schmidt helped launch me on this enduring journey, going all the way back to a time when we envisioned the creation of Tooradin Writers' Week and made it a reality for young writers and their teachers. Barry always brought a can-do attitude that extended my own vision of what was possible for this teacher who wrote.

Thank you also to all the teachers, principals, school communities, ALEA (Australian Literacy Educators' Association) members and fellow education consultants who support my work to this very day, especially Lisa Burman, Anne Babich, Helen Chatto, Alex Artavilla, Meg Dallas, Ken Ryan, Glen Knight and Diane Snowball, educational leaders who showed faith in my work and afforded me opportunities to share critical messages about writing pedagogy.

To valued friends Colin Murray, Rob Jones, Peter Hayne and Shane O'Brien: thank you for your wise counsel and timely support. It has sustained me immeasurably.

I also thank fellow educational writers the late Donald Graves, Ralph Fletcher, Katie Wood Ray and Matt Glover for the light they have shone into the educational landscape – a light that has frequently sustained my writing endeavours.

This book owes its existence to all of you.

INITIAL THOUGHTS

I took this photograph in Rome on Via del Pellegrino, close to the famous produce market, Campo de' Fiori. Upon returning home to Australia, I had the photo enlarged, and now it sits prominently on a wall in my home.

It reminds me that one does not develop as a cyclist merely by looking at a picture of a bicycle. No, we must clamber onto said two-wheeled contraption and push off on our perilous first journey. It may be short-lived and may involve a sudden ending.

Our first efforts are most likely accompanied by a high degree of uncertainty and white-knuckled gripping of the handlebars. We wobble and shake in our desperate attempts to control the direction of the seemingly unmanageable conveyance. Our efforts are concentrated towards making those wilful wheels travel in a straight line, avoiding potential hazards such as fences, potholes, power poles – people!

Learning to ride a bicycle may also involve a few mishaps. It is most unusual not to experience the occasional 'prang' – the kind of accident that separates rider and bicycle and occasions cuts, scrapes and a few bruises. A bit of *bark* off our knees comes with the terrain the rider is exploring.

Despite such setbacks, the inexperienced rider generally persists, and a measure of control begins to develop. The bicycle yields to the will of a determined rider. Eventually the ability to swerve around some unsuspecting pedestrian, an errant dog, a muddy puddle, a tree or another cyclist emerges and the journey becomes more controlled, more predictable, less angst-ridden (pardon the pun).

I frequently find myself reminding young writers of these facts and drawing an analogy with learning to write. Wobbly at first, the writer starts out with great uncertainty and a lack of control. Through practice, persistence and good old-fashioned stickability, the writer develops greater confidence and control over the direction the writing takes.

This is a message we not only share with developing student writers, it's a message for all writers, regardless of age. I continue to meet a significant number of teachers who wish to know about being more effective as teachers of writing. They question the effectiveness of their current practice. However, many of them do not write by choice. Their students do not view them as writers. There is an obvious disconnect between what they wish to achieve and what their current practice as teachers of writing looks like. If teachers are prepared to write alongside their students, they will grow to understand how writers think and what writers need. They will grow to understand and appreciate the joys and the struggles that accompany writing. The pictures in their head will be forever changed.

There is little danger in not being a writer in the physical sense. Most people are not writers and not much harm results from that fact. You don't hear of them being stoned to death with popcorn or sentenced to ten years in the electric chair for their sin of omission. However, I much prefer the genuine uncertainty and chance discovery derived from a world swirling with dangerous, daring words. Many times, I have emerged from that amazing world smiling broadly with a survivor's joy. Words excite me.

The message here is a simple one: just as you did all those years ago, climb back onto the bike and start pedalling. On your bike, squire. There you go…

Brave writers (and bike riders) can be any age. It just requires daring. The writer embraces the invitation offered by the blank page and covers it gradually with words. In this way the writer asserts freedom and the power to act. Initial words lead to more words. The journey is under way. A bit like riding a bike actually. Off we go!

1

DANCES WITH WORDS

I launched my first writer's notebook way back in 1983 with the following wonderings:

> What should I include? I am unsure, having somewhat limited knowledge of notebooks… Should I write as the mood takes me? Schemes, dreams, visions, reflections and related stories? All, I hope. My hope is that the interest in this notebook will grow, just like my interest in gardening and growing things. If it provides a similar form of therapy and inspiration, I'll be well pleased.
>
> The task of writing is ever new – a process of discovery. I have a strong leaning towards writing about my childhood experiences. This involves a process of rediscovery.
>
> 'When you start slowly, you practise slowly, but you learn fast.' So said D'Artagnan of musketeer fame. I'm not sure if he said that, but those words were assigned to him in a film script. I hope you're right, D'Artagnan.

In the beginning I maintained a single notebook, but now I have several notebooks developing simultaneously, and for different purposes. I have a large writer's notebook that is used in my work as an educational consultant and writer. This notebook travels with me each day, when I visit schools. It is an essential part of my working kit. As the man in the suit said many years ago in the advertisement for American Express, 'Don't leave home without it!' He wasn't actually referring to a writer's notebook, but the words resonate strongly when preparing for each day's work. Car keys, wallet, phone, a book to read, writer's notebook. It's that important. It is a trusted travelling companion. It jumps into my bag anytime I venture beyond our house. It's a kind of insurance in case an opportunity presents. I write in this notebook at home as well.

I write in a writer's notebook because I need a safe place for my fragile first words. A place where those words will be initially protected from harsh and premature judgment. I think of my notebook as one would a garden. I hope that things planted there will grow and flourish.

As a child, I was fascinated by pirate stories and the escapades of Long John Silver and Captain Blood. As a writer, I can become a little piratical with the pen and the page.

I am conscious my notebook will be read by students, so to some extent this influences the types of entries gathered within its pages. When I travel overseas, I generally take what I refer to as my traveller's notebook. It is a smaller, slimmer volume, suitable for packing into my luggage. Its compact size is ideal for the adventures associated with travel. The writing in this notebook is decidedly more scrawled, as I am usually the only one who reads this notebook. I enjoy writing about travel experiences, and this notebook traps a wide range of observations gathered from a world of infinite wonders. One summer, I wrote in a notebook aimed at capturing the experiences and perceptions of the warmest season. It too was a small volume, graciously given to me by a teacher and her class of young writers. The gift inspired me to write exclusively across the summer in a notebook dedicated to that purpose. I also have a notebook for my musical memories across the years. Music has been a constant refrain through my life and therefore deserves a dedicated space. It's an occasional notebook. Entries are added as they come to mind.

Choice begins with selecting the notebook that best works for you, the writer. Since starting out with that first notebook, I have filled many more with words and wonderings. They have provided me with ideas and directions for a variety of writing projects across time. They have continued to develop and change over the years as I have. They have entered my writing life in varying shapes and sizes as I searched for the most comfortable format. A format suited to me, personally. Like my life, the notebooks I use continue to evolve. I have found a way of working with a writer's notebook that suits me. It's not 'the' way to work with a notebook, it's my way.

I am well prepared for my writing future. On the shelves in my study sits a collection of future notebooks from which to choose. Like a squirrel gathers acorns, I gather notebooks. Among the collected reserves are impressive leather-bound examples with recycled paper, the famed Moleskine notebooks of different dimensions and a recent acquisition that features a rather eye-catching cover made from recycled plastic. It already possesses a sense of individuality. They announce themselves to me in stationery shops, specialty gift shops, newsagencies and office supply outlets. I am not sure if their numbers are increasing in such places or if I am just more aware of them. I would like to think that it is a case of the former. Irrespective of the actual answer, I have effectively taken out insurance. I have made an optimistic statement regarding my continuing writing intentions.

I remember as a child being a great collector of things. I collected marbles of different colours and designs. I collected football cards, toy soldiers and animals. I collected unusual stones, glass, ball bearings and elastic bands, anything that caught my eye or felt good when held in my hand. I recall gathering a sizable collection of books, comics and magazines. I had a big collection of Little Golden Books as part of my personal library. As an adult, I still collect things. The focus of my collecting these days is books, music, sea-glass, shirts and cameras. It is this history of being a collector that explains why I use my writer's notebook as a collection zone for words and ideas. I gather up photos, notes, ephemera, trivia and facts, observations, drawings, maps, quotes and news items and collect them inside the covers of my notebooks. I am an avid harvester of words. I note that this tendency to collect is a common characteristic of many artists, designers and fellow writers. I feel I am in good company.

My writer's notebook is not an artist's sketchbook, nor a scrapbook. It's not a diary or a journal, but it often contains elements of all the previously mentioned repositories. However, the fact that we refer to it as a 'writer's' notebook suggests that the main ingredient should in fact be – writing!

It is also true that not every writer maintains a writer's notebook, but a significant number of writers do! These notebooks come in different shapes and sizes, just as people do. The configurations of these writers' notebooks are as diverse as the authors who own them. The aim is to configure the notebook in such a way that your individual preferences can shine through as the notebook develops.

My notebooks are many and varied. Lined and unlined. Thick and thin. Large and small. When it comes to their covers, the uniqueness of each notebook receives sharp focus. The acquisition of each new notebook presents an opportunity for the writer to stamp their individuality upon the notebook's outer face. It is at this stage that a range of options comes the writer's way. The writer's role as decision maker comes to the fore. I freely admit to enjoying creating a unique cover for each notebook in need of identity markers.

Occasionally I choose to leave the cover unadorned. I figure the cover as presented is striking enough. One notebook I received as a gift from my wife was purchased from Manufactus, a wonderful notebook shop in the heart of Rome. It would have been sacrilege to add anything to the notebook's rich, black leather cover. The notebook possessed an inherent beauty and, when held in my hand, unique appeal. Its authentic, leathery smell was intoxicating. Its handmade-paper pages invited the spread of freshly scribed words.

Many of my notebook covers have been decorated with an assortment of materials, though. Magazine cut-outs, selected photographs, headlines, quotes and stickers have been appropriated to create a personal collage. I always enjoy organising and shaping the various element into a pleasing, hopefully eye-catching arrangement before gluing the pieces into their assigned places. When we decide to personalise our notebook covers, we immediately assume ownership of that notebook, endowing it with unique characteristics. These various additions are designed to make a statement regarding our personal interests and identity as writers. The work of scissors, glue and personal choice is integral in this process of personalisation.

It is also possible to create a collage cover electronically and then print it off before gluing it onto the notebook. I designed a traditional bookplate and used that as my personalised cover on one notebook. I enjoyed the creative process that this entailed.

I must admit, I generally like to decorate the back of my notebooks too. I like them to be totally mine. Each notebook is presented to the world as my notebook, not to be confused with anyone else's. I think to myself at the conclusion of montage manoeuvres, 'Well, that pretty much covers it…'

I am aware that there are a multitude of writers who choose not to personalise any of their notebook covers – ever. Some writers select the same type of notebook every time because that style of notebook suits their individual needs. For them, variety is less important than comfort and familiarity. We must each find what works best for us.

My notebook provides a place to be honest. It is a place free of critics. In his book *Breathing In, Breathing Out*, Ralph Fletcher (1996a) describes a notebook thus: 'Your notebook is a room of your own. It encourages you to inhabit the first-person pronoun and without apology.'

My notebook is a place where discoveries take place. I frequently notice I have more to say about a particular subject or idea than I originally believed. The act of writing has allowed this realisation to emerge.

My notebooks contain the truth of my existence – at least a version of that truth – and in that truth, I am given the rare opportunity to discover the treasure a life possesses. When I mine my thoughts, ideas and wonderings, so many affirming possibilities emerge.

My book *Igniting Writing: When a Teacher Writes* (Wright, 2011) grew largely from notebook entries harvested from my notebooks. My poetry anthologies, *Searching for Hen's Teeth* (Wright, 2014) and *I Bet There's No Broccoli on the Moon* (Wright, 2016) grew from poems lifted from notebooks across a lifetime of poetry entries. I mined the pages in search of possibilities, lifted the raw words and polished them for publication. There were casualties – entries that didn't make the cut. Because I had played with words on a regular basis, there were plentiful poetic possibilities. My options were enhanced.

I have no way of ever knowing whether the accumulated notebook entries will prove to be of any importance to those who may review my raw words at some time in the future. They may wonder what prompted them, who knows? It's for me that I write. Initially, it's for me to understand the gathered words. I do know I am writing to save my life. That sounds overly dramatic, but it is the recording of these life experiences that ensures my journey is documented. It is my time, my songlines, my truth. My notebook is central to my writing life. If I don't write, my tiny place in history slowly evaporates like morning mist.

I am reminded of the famous question frequently asked of mountaineers. Why do you climb mountains? Because they're there! Thomas Berger (n.d.) wrote, 'Writers write because it isn't there.' That's good enough for me.

It is claimed that writing takes you away, isolates you from the world. My notebook life has increased my awareness of my world. So, as much as the time I spend lost in my notebook takes me away, it has hopefully strengthened my connections to others through the insights it has provided. My notebook is like a garden. If I continue to feed it, things will flourish.

I fondly recall my father's devotion to his extensive vegetable garden. The bounty he harvested over many years was stunning proof of his considerable investment. When family and friends dropped by our house, my father was able to offer them fresh fruit and vegetables carefully grown in his garden. The garden consumed his time, but that time was productively used. He would return with a bounty that he willingly shared with others.

My notebook life has taught me many things. Firstly, to trust my thoughts and to use words prolifically to make discoveries. I have become less fearful in my writing. As Aimee Buckner (2005) notes in *Notebook Knowhow*:

> If a notebook is to be a useful tool however, it must be useful to the writer first and the reader second. The creation of each notebook is in the hands of the writer.

My work in schools regularly incorporates the use of writers' notebooks. Student writers in these schools (using notebooks as a resource) are thankfully afforded authentic choice to develop their writing. Consequently, their writing voices emerge. The efforts of their teachers clearly support the efforts of these inexperienced writers. Their reflections are most instructive:

> To me, a writer's notebook isn't something you have to do, but something you choose to do. A writer's notebook is where we can express what has been boxed in for so long and share it on a page. It is where we have our own opinion and our own unique style. Words just flow out onto the page. There are no limits when we write. There is no time frame. *(Eleni, Grade 6)*

> Keeping my ideas trapped in my mind is an illness. My writer's notebook is my rescuer. Writing is my life, but there's a door in front of it. My writer's notebook is the key to open it. *(Christian, Grade 5)*

A writer's notebook doesn't have a voice. The words you write in the notebook give it a voice. When I was six, I began to write about the relationship between my mum and dad. I still do.

I love my writer's notebook. Everything I write, I try and make it come from my heart. Whenever I feel upset or worried, I must write it down, just to let it out or remember it. *(Desire, Grade 6)*

What do I like to write about you ask?

Daring knights, beautiful princesses, ferocious dragons, trolls, tall castles, crazy foods, odd characters, peculiar places and anything else to do with fantasy. That's why my writer's notebook is special to me. I can write about anything, absolutely anything. My writer's notebook lets my imagination go free without anyone telling me I can't do that. *(Georgia, Grade 5)*

CONSIDER

A writer's notebook is a place to be a risk taker. A writing space where you can indulge in some derring-do as a writer. A place where, as a writer, you can indulge in a degree of experimental action with words and ideas without external judgment.

The very act of writing stimulates creativity. The pieces that grow within the covers of a notebook are invaluable to a writer. As we write, we learn to value the words gathering in that special place. Those words will hopefully form the foundation of longer pieces that may emerge later. Arise rebel writer!

2

COLLECTING THE RAW STUFF

What I think and feel before I write is frequently attached to memories and thoughts gathered in my mind. I need to sort them out in order to get them on the page. To satisfy the needs of a potential reader, I must flesh out my thoughts into something more substantial. Rehearsal is an essential part of that process, yet even with rehearsal what often first lands on the line are thoughts and fragments I would classify as raw stuff, words requiring additional attention.

My writer's notebook has become an essential part of my writing identity – a collection zone for ideas and experiences, a safe place to experiment and take risks, a resource for teaching. Like the words actor Karl Malden famously uttered in an iconic advertisement for American Express way back in 1975, when it comes to my notebook, *I don't leave home without it*. More than four decades of raw stuff have been gathered across the pages of assorted notebooks in that time.

I do not keep a writer's notebook. It keeps me. It keeps me writing. It keeps me thinking. It keeps me closely observing my world. As Ernest Hemingway (1964) stated, 'I belong to this notebook and this pencil.' I do not write in my notebook every single day. However, I certainly write most days and, on the days when I don't write, I am usually considering what I want to write next. I cannot stay away. My notebook beckons to me like the Sirens called Ulysses.

None of my notebooks would be considered a journal or a diary. They are quite clearly notebooks, meant for the collective random gatherings of my life and the sometimes uniquely wired world inside my head. Something pops out and I feel the strong compulsion to write it down just in case I need it later. Fleeting thoughts sit comfortably alongside thoroughly considered comments. All features of great and small…

Creative bursts of reflection and scattered recollections are haphazardly scattered across the hungry pages of my notebook. I do not use sections in my notebooks. Nor do I number pages or keep an index. I tried these things once and they only brought on frustration. So now I give my thoughts free rein. Entries are recorded in the order they arrive.

Across the vast stretch of time that writers' notebooks have been part of my existence as a writer, they have come in many forms. Lined and unlined, thick and thin, large and small. None of them had spiral-bound spines. All of them had strong covers. My notebooks must be robust, hardy and durable. It's a tough existence for a working notebook.

Some writers use their notebooks to brainstorm ideas. Some fill notebooks with observations that eventually form the foundations of larger writing projects. Other writers use their notebooks to record their writing progress while undertaking a writing project. Some writers simultaneously conduct multiple notebooks for different purposes. I must admit I have done this too. At one time I kept my poetry in a separate notebook, and I used another notebook exclusively for writing about music. Notebooks are unique to that writer. There is no 'one way' that notebooks must be 'done'.

There are many orthodoxies that develop around notebooks, and we should be wary of them. The notebook should not become a chore, something that must be done every single day without fail. The notebook should be fun to be around – always ready to capture the gatherings of its owner/writer. It is not a task that must be done. It is a place of wonder and possibility. The collection zone for the storing of potential writing projects. A place for fact and fantasy, experimentation and imagination. No one else should presume to take away the ownership of your notebook. It is most certainly a place to write. A place to create beginnings, plans, notes, and first drafts. It might also be a place to draw, sketch maps and make lists. It is, above all, a place to harvest your own unique endeavours and interests.

Your notebook provides a space in which you can feel free to wander. A place to be silly or serious depending on your mood. You may poke about in the darker recesses of your mind or reflect in the brightest light. Keep your notebook close by. Feed it regularly. Be responsible for its continued good health. Let it becomes a natural part of your creative life. When you look at the collective pages of your notebook entries, you are privileged to see the footprints of your life and times.

Every time I pick up a pen to write, the rest of my world defaults to standby. Everything else comes to a halt. Only the writing matters.

Mel Levine (2003), in *The Myth of Laziness*, describes writing as 'exquisite synchronisation'. At this point my mind is pried open and thoughts begin to flow. I am connected only to the page. The invitation of the blank page takes over and must be respectfully responded to, immediately. The first words to spill onto the pages of a notebook are often raw and untamed. It doesn't all glitter. As writers, we just want to trap those thoughts and ideas before they evade us. To do this, we must carve out some time to write, set time aside to allow our writing to develop. We must learn to quarantine time in our hectic lives. We must give life to the writing ideas that come calling. Maybe beginning with things we never want to forget.

For writing to move beyond good intentions, a degree of self-indulgence is required. Conscious self-indulgence, if you like. Remove the roadblocks inhibiting your writing. Writing is an act of problem-solving. No one knows better than you what these obstacles are. Get them out of the way! Out damn spot!

For this to happen, writing must be treated as something important – a task too important, too urgent to be ignored. Prioritise, even if it takes you away from other tasks. Make time to breathe life into your words. Commit to the act of writing. Gather the raw stuff. Gather it regularly. Writing is all about the forming of a habit. Writers are not born; they are created by action and deed.

Habits require time to develop. Automaticity is unique to each of us, but it is the regular repetition of the action that enables the habit to form.

We need a cue. A notebook kept in a prominent place perhaps. We need the behaviour (find a convenient place and time – and write!) and the reward that arises from accomplishing the task of writing. The visible representation of your words on the page. This raw material is full of potential. First, we harvest it, then we examine it to assess its value.

Quarantining Time for Writing

Many years ago, I read a book called *Dear Writer* by Carmel Bird (1988). The book presented a series of letters to aspiring writers, offering hope and inspiration as well as sobering advice. I recall how the author urged her adult student writers to learn to quarantine time for writing. Writers must learn to be a little wickedly self-indulgent, Bird wrote. She then went further and urged fellow writers to give up nearly all the housework. She claimed it was a clear choice between a clean house and a finished story.

Such radical action makes the indulgent writer unpopular with family and friends and is not something that I could commit to, but it does highlight an immediate issue for those of us who choose to write.

Some working days I am alone in the house. It may be a preparation day before the working week unfolds. Following breakfast, some household task keeps calling and the bed-making cannot be put off any longer, and all the time I am doing these tasks I am thinking about the writing and the planning I need to do as well. I still must take my morning walk, and the dishwasher needs emptying.

I aim to clear the decks relatively quickly to create time for the words that have been swirling wildly in my head. Writers spend as much time rehearsing their words as they spend churning them out, or as a student writer wrote 'inking them onto the page'. I must be honest. I am not totally committed to household duties. I lack the zeal required for spotlessness. Occasionally, I give in, and the writing is given priority. It regularly consumes a large chunk of the day. Then, I rush madly about to get the housework done before my dear wife returns, tired at her working day's end.

Such days present temptations, but they also present realities. After all, it's a balancing act between indulging a passion and being a contributor in the immediate life of your family. I am a member of more than one team. When I am in the cave (alternative name for my study) writing, I may devote myself to the task until the washing machine cycle ends and the clothes demand to be pegged on the line. They want to make the most of the day's glorious sunshine. It's tough having two masters. I can hear Carmel Bird's voice, but I'm just not that brave, or crazy, or selfish.

The world is full of people with good intentions. These people are gunners! They are always 'gunna' do this or do that. They say things like, 'One day I'm gunna try skydiving. One day I'm gunna travel. One day I'm gunna write my memoirs. One day I'm gunna chop that tree down. One day I'm gunna build a replica of the *Endeavour*. Trouble is, they never quite reach the point of committing. Sorry, writing requires action heroes.

Location, Location, Location...

Writing is mostly a solitary endeavour. However, for writing to emerge, the writer needs to feel comfortable. I mostly write in the relative peace of my study. When I am there, I am in my preferred writing space.

However, I also have times when I like to write surrounded by the noisy orchestra of life. At these times I don't need the cone of silence surrounding me. When this happens, I will seek out a coffee shop, a library or any other convenient location. Because I spend a lot of time in schools, I often find a few spare minutes to write somewhere in the school. That's the value of having my notebook with me. I can maximise the moment, wherever it might present itself. In these noisier environments, I can still focus on my thoughts, push back the distractions and just write. Writing, like reading, is a form of portable magic. With a notebook close to hand, I can write any time, anywhere.

Ronald T. Kellogg (1994) in *The Psychology of Writing* states:

> There is evidence that environments, schedules and rituals restructure the writing process and amplify performance... The room, time of day or ritual selected for working may enable or even induce intense concentration or a favourable motivational or emotional state.

From personal experience, I have found this to be true. We must each find our own optimum conditions for writing, our preferred locations. Some writers try to eliminate all sounds for fear of distraction. Noisy locations raise their anxiety. The sudden intrusion of noise in an otherwise quiet location may also raise anxiety. I am particularly thrown by lawnmowers, leaf blowers and edge trimmers suddenly starting up. I am more than content for the grass to grow while I am engaged in writing.

While some writers embrace sound, others may find the ticking of a clock distracting yet feel perfectly at ease writing in a busy café. Cafés don't faze me as a rule. I can create a strong connection to my notebook despite the hubbub around me. With a coffee, a pen and a notebook, I can focus while those around me converse.

Some writers feel the need to write exclusively indoors, while others can write quite comfortably in the fresh air. I occasionally write beside the sea, or in a park. The vast majority of my writing, though, takes place in my study. It is set up to facilitate my personal writing processes.

My research into writing spaces revealed that renowned author Roald Dahl set up his writing space in a 'shed' located away from his house (Blake, 2008). The interior of this dedicated space was organised totally as a place for writing. Dahl preferred to write on yellow legal paper, using his favourite pencils. In a jar beside him were six yellow pencils – always six. He would sit in a large chair and place a large felt-covered board made from plywood across his lap. He assembled books, a sturdy old lamp, a large wastepaper basket and some filing cabinets. A red thermos of coffee was also at hand to keep him alert through the night.

He would step into a sleeping bag pulled up to his waist to ward off the cold. To his right stood a table upon which Dahl would arrange a display of artefacts and assorted memorabilia – including a piece of his own hip bone removed in an operation. Among the gathered oddments adorning the table was a ball of silver paper collected from chocolate bars dating back to when he was a small boy, shells, jars, a coffee mug, scissors, handwritten notes, framed photographs, an electric pencil-sharpener and items sent to him by fans of his writing. Dahl had created a space specific to his needs, and look what came from that. From the most predictable environments, the most unpredictable things can arise.

My search through Roald Dahl's writing shed alerted me to my own personal writing space. My interest piqued, I scanned my study, slowly and deliberately. I too have assembled an assortment of items connected to both my writing and my broader life. I found it fascinating to think how unconsciously this had occurred. Items are scattered across the shelves, not gathered on a table, but they are numerous and visible. They sit beside treasured books, magazines, assorted writers' notebooks, a filing cabinet and writing materials to sustain my writing efforts. Unlike Dahl, my study embraces modern technology, with a scanner, a printer and a desktop computer taking up prominent positions alongside my more traditional writing resources – paper, pens and glue sticks – the noble tools of a writer.

Renowned Australian author Tim Winton (2015) prefers a totally different space. He writes about his preferred surroundings in *Island Home*. Tim writes, 'I can't even hang a painting in my workroom, for what else is a painting, but a window… so for a lot of the time I write in a blank cubicle, my back to the view.'

I too write with my back to the view, but I am not distracted by my surrounding bookshelves. The words of authors in the books around me often whisper gentle advice. I sense their presence, and it sustains me. Their counsel is close by if needed. Every writer has a unique way of structuring the writing space, and each writer has their foibles.

For the photograph below, I gathered some of the artefacts scattered around my study. Each of them is important to me. Each of them has a particular story or memory attached. Not all my memorabilia are represented here – but a considerable collection. Just like my notebooks, the collected items are unique to me, the owner and the gatherer. They provide a certain comfort in my preferred writing space.

Writers perform their essential work of bringing words to the page in a host of locations. In the end, it matters little where one writes; it is more important to feel comfortable in that chosen space. How and where you write is less important than what you write.

Time After Time

Time on task is important. How else do we develop our writing stamina? Because writing is an effective way to develop thinking, it is important to create time for our writing stamina to develop. When we begin to engage in regular, sustained writing, we signal to the world that writing is valued. For teachers, this critical message must be at the very front of their thinking when working with student writers.

Some people like music playing while they work. It's something I do occasionally. The conditions required for writing to occur are a personal thing. It takes time and a degree of trial and error to find what circumstances best support you to write. What are the optimum conditions for you to be focused as a writer?

Ernest Hemingway explained his optimum writing conditions in an interview in 1958:

> When I am working on a book or a story, I write every morning as soon after first light as possible. There is no one to disturb you and it is cool or cold, and you come to your work and warm as you write. You read what you have written and, as you always stop when you know what is going to happen next, you go from there. You write until you come to a place where you still have your juice and know what will happen next and you stop and try to live through until morning when you hit it again. You have started at six in the morning, say, and may go on until noon or be through before that. *(Paris Review, interview conducted by George Plimpton, 1958)*

The ingredients that facilitate writing need to be associated with a preferred time and place for each individual writer. When we enter our preferred writing environment, the relevant behaviour is cued, and from there the writing flows. The challenge remains to develop your writing rituals and link them to a preferred time and place. Thinking can take place anywhere. The secret lies in finding an environment that allows concentrated participation in the writing task. Developing the habit of writing is the key that launches a writing life.

Sometimes writing, or more particularly the discipline surrounding it, can be elusive. There are days when my words flow freely onto the page. The stark whiteness of the page surrenders easily to my words – my will. There are also those days when I feel I am pushing the words out. The flow stutters and the ideas are somewhat faltering. I accept this ebb and flow of inspiration. It's the reality of writing. I never hide this fact from the teachers and students with whom I work. It would be dishonest. There are days when writing is plain hard work, and there are other days when it is pure joy. In this way writing is a mirror of our broader lives.

Writing Away from Home

I love it when a writing kind of day comes along. I might find myself sitting in my favourite coffee haunt. If I'm lucky, I might be able to access my favourite seat where I can write without disruption. With a cappuccino and my current notebook, I am set up to compose. I listen to the voices of customers and staff. I might gaze out the window at the passing parade. Sidewalk tables are occupied; shoppers float past; cars, trucks and bicycles slowly cruise by.

I will stay here for up to an hour seeking words and ideas, embedded as I am in the buzz and hum of this small café. The numbers ebb and flow, the noise rises and falls in a kind of rhythm. In a broader working life these moments are precious. This is the world beyond my usual work locations. I savour these experiences. They remind me that a writer must be out in the world in order to fully understand the rituals of daily life. My senses are heightened in this place. I attend to the competing sounds, trying to consciously isolate them in my mind. Neil Finn's voice floats across the café as coffee beans spill loudly into the grinder:

> Tell me all the things you would change
> I don't pretend to know what you want
> When you come around and spin my top
> Time and again, time and again
>
> ('Distant Sun', Neil Finn)

Coins jangle in the register as another customer pays for their morning coffee fix. I hear the sharp clanking of china cups and the clatter of saucers being arranged behind the counter. The coffee machine emits a loud hiss – a sigh of relief. Such are the orchestral manoeuvres of the coffee shop. There is energy in this place – it feeds my writing. Soon I will address more mundane issues like visiting the supermarket and returning home to prepare for more writing and tomorrow's work, but just for now, let me linger in the café's soothing embrace. I sip my coffee, open my notebook and the words floating and tumbling in my head begin to flow across the pages of my notebook.

Savouring the Moment

Writing does not always concern itself with big issues. Beauty can be found in writing more specifically about the smaller slices of our lives. Writing accurately and honestly about life experiences takes the reader below the surface, affording them a greater appreciation of the simple observations contained in the text. It is a backstage pass. Ralph Fletcher (1992), in his book *What a Writer Needs*, states, 'The writing becomes more beautiful when it becomes more specific.' We, who choose to write, would do well to remember this important piece of information.

Stories often emerge from small moments in which there is only enough time to perform a brief task or action. Think of things that happen in your life that, while taking only a moment of your day, can nonetheless assume importance. These slices of our lives make great fodder for writing if we allow them into our writing consciousness.

I frequently talk to student writers about making stronger connections to the wonders of the world surrounding them. I impress upon them that writers of all ages need to be observers, collectors and eavesdroppers. On one such occasion a young Grade 5 writer offered the following remark: 'Well, we have been living in the same house for years now and I've only just noticed that we have a hole in our laundry wall.' This revelation suddenly emerged as if propelled to the edge of consciousness by our discussion. While we all appreciated the humour of the moment, it illustrated how something can be right in front of us and we just don't see it.

In this instance all present were duly informed that a fellow writer was announcing her increased awareness of her immediate surroundings. Hopefully, she will begin to make more significant discoveries because of her new sense of vision. All writers need to look closely at their immediate environment and see the potential for writing ideas.

Searching for and seeking out the wonder in small things, chance encounters and small moments provides a rich source of ideas for the writer to feed their notebook. The collecting of ideas flows more effortlessly from this point. Here are two such moments that found their way into my notebooks.

> *Summer Morning in the Garden*
>
> Summer mornings possess a special quality. In that brief cooler part of the day before the sun climbs to its full height and intensity, the vapours of the earth slowly rise and mingle with the assorted scents of the garden. Plants glisten with dewy deposits; the day is at its peak of freshness. A constant chorus of birdsong celebrates the wonder of the new day. Bees, dragonflies and assorted small creatures begin their daily routines. I stand there, as the life of the garden stirs into action. It is such an easy pleasure to celebrate a summer morning. It has been an unusually wet summer. Record rainfall and humidity have been features of the season. I stand on the decking with a cup of tea and survey the scene of our small garden. The garden has a dankness – dewy and drippy. The aromas mingle. Such a fecund marvellous moment…

Homing in on the Huntsman

Following a chance conversation with a group of young writers investigating a range of creepy-crawlies, I began to think about the common Australian Huntsman spiders and their characteristics. That brief encounter had sparked my interest and a need to write. It activated my prior knowledge; I began by listing what I already knew in my notebook.

My list included:

- They move very quickly.
- The female lays up to 200 eggs.
- They don't build webs.
- They have eight large, long hairy legs.
- Flattened bodies are ideal for living in narrow spaces.
- They are crab-like and grow up to 15 centimetres from leg to leg.
- People often refer to them erroneously as 'tarantulas'.
- They have no qualms about entering houses and cars.

Anecdotally, I knew they often announce their presence by scurrying across the windscreen or dashboard, or just suddenly dropping from the sun visor.

I felt compelled to explore further and began researching this unusual arachnid. I discovered they often take over burrows discarded by other creatures, such as cicadas. They also shed their skin. Huntsman spiders are not aggressive, and a bite usually causes inconvenience that can be treated with an ice pack, so their physical appearance is misleading.

I moved on to other spiders of which I had some knowledge. I began investigating such species as the garden orb weaver and the deadly redback spider, both common in Australia. By now my mind was racing with spidery possibilities.

The result of all this research was the beginning of a writing project – a narrative concerning a spider named Harriet…

> A long thin hairy leg emerges from beneath a rusty sheet of corrugated iron. That single leg is followed by seven more legs belonging to Harriet the spider. Harriet is a Huntsman spider and very proud of the fact…

We'll see where this leads. I am indebted to the conversation I had with those young writers. A spark was ignited, and I was drawn to it. Notebook time and some extra reading opened more writing opportunities.

SPIDERS

Huntsman Spiders have no qualms about entering houses. They often seem to come inside just before an approaching storm. People often think their appearance inside a house is a sign that rain is coming.

Huntsman seem to love entering cars too. They announce their sudden presence by scurrying across the dashboard.

Huntsman are found throughout Australia.

Huntsman shed their skin in order to grow. Sometimes I have found discarded old skin and thought it was a spider.

I didn't know that they often take over the discarded burrows of cicadas.

Huntsman Spiders are mostly grey to brown in colour. They are large with long hairy legs.

They have flattened bodies ideal for living in narrow spaces. They are very crab like.

Australian Huntsman Spiders are often called 'tarantulas' when sighted on house walls. They terrify people when they scuttle out from behind curtains.

* If you get bitten by a Huntsman - a cold ice pack may ease the pain.

My Research Revealed:
- They move very quickly
- The female lays up to 200 eggs.
- They can measure up to 15 cms - leg to leg
- They have 8 eyes
- As adults they do not build webs

Writing in a World of Wonders

In the John Prine song 'Angel from Montgomery' Bonnie Raitt's evocative voice sings:

> But how the hell can a person
> Go on to work in the morning
> To come home in the evening
> And have nothing to say.

In these words there exists a profound sadness. It is a story of people we have all encountered at some stage in our lives. Too many people experience their worldly existence in this way. They present as undernourished souls. Their days drift by. They appear to mean nothing. The new day holds no demonstrable attraction. Desensitised to the world around them, these diminished souls live a life detached from the abundant rich pickings that surround daily existence. Opportunities slide by. Opportunities to enjoy simple pleasures don't register. A bland existence is their dubious prize. They have stopped reacting to their world.

After 16 years living in the same house, we moved to a new house, in a different part of the same neighbourhood. To connect more fully with our new surroundings, I increased the amount of walking I was doing. I deliberately chose to walk in different directions, taking different routes, while gradually increasing the duration of these walks. Apart from the obvious health benefits, my awareness of the immediate area grew each time I ventured forth. These little adventures engaged my senses: the voices of people going about their daily lives, the beauty and fragrance of the local flora, the sounds of magpies chortling, the feel of the lavender bushes, the crunch of dry summer grasses under my feet, the lingering aromas of onions frying on a barbecue floating over tall fences, the salty air of the sea floating over the headland and the hissing of the wind through the eucalypts along the esplanade.

Walking along the esplanade overlooking the bay, I found myself captivated by the intensity of the sapphirine ocean. The morning light displayed the water at its brilliant best. I was privileged to see dolphins chasing a school of fry through the shallows. They dived and romped directly off the beach, and the assembled witnesses ooh-ed and aah-ed in unison each time the dolphins leapt in the air. A quicksilver moment.

Dog walkers, beach-bound teens, towels slung over their shoulders, bike-riders surging up hills, the intoxicating smell of coffee as I walked by the nearby Lilo Café – I was awake to it all. I ran my hand over the smooth trunk of a ghost gum. I marvelled at the vivid purple of the lush bougainvillea in the nearby laneway. A peacock of a plant, it dazzled with intensity. I noticed the shapes of shadows on the footpath as I passed. On those mornings when the summer air was windless, I walked in hope of sensing a breeze. All those phenomena to be experienced, noticed, appreciated, enjoyed. I celebrated my good fortune. I soaked in the sights. I was awake to them, ready to receive their immeasurable bounty. Their presence in my life continues to nourish and sustain me. I breathe them in, ever thankful to be tuned in to the part they play in my sense of wellbeing. I walk most mornings, consciously taking a different route each time. Surprise me world. Surprise me morning…

My writing life is profoundly enriched by these experiences. Vicki, my wife, called out to me one morning, 'Al, come quickly, come quickly, you don't want to miss this!' Her voice was laced with urgency. I responded straightaway. I trust her observational abilities implicitly. She pointed to a faint rectangular shadow on the wall outside the study. It quivered almost imperceptibly, this moving picture. The image of thin tree branches projected onto the wall in delicate shadows greeted us, fragile, fleeting and beautifully framed. Another simple pleasure shared. We stood in admiration. That's as it should be.

It is increasingly apparent that many kids go on trips in the family car equipped with DVD players, iPads and other techno wizardry. It is also apparent that many of them see little beyond a screen. They fail to notice the passing parade of natural and man-made wonders, simply because their eyes are kept captive inside the vehicle. They only have eyes for the screen. Their world view is severely limited in every sense. I am fearful they may grow up to be the kinds of people Bonnie Raitt sings about.

Teachers now experience added pressure to ensure their classrooms are full of wonder and curiosity about the world within and beyond the classroom walls. It begins with the teacher and what they value, what they bring with them. So much of teaching is about engagement and provocation. Thinking and questioning. Noticing details, valuing small moments. The developing learner (the developing writer) needs this stimulation to launch the essential creative processes to foster and grow a curious learner.

In many ways teaching is about compensating for the gaps in a learner's experience. In classrooms where thinking and inquiry are pursued and quality conversations are the norm, curious learners are nurtured. When a teacher makes it a priority to share personal connections to the infinite wonders of the world, they are shining a light into what might have been a previously unlit space in a child's mind.

Upon entering classrooms, I frequently commence by asking the assembled student writers: 'What did you see this week that amazed you?' Initially, I don't get much of a response, so I open my writer's notebook and begin to share some of the observational entries I have gathered: drawings, photographs, news clippings, and assorted writing. As writers, we must be observers and collectors, I tell them. Curious learners start to rouse. They want to know more. The back story slowly becomes important to them: 'Who? What? When? Why? How?' they ask. Follow-up visits begin with the same question, and in little time they start to volunteer their own observations and recordings with an eagerness. They want me to know about their amazing discoveries. The spark has been lit...

'This week a bird flew into our yard; I had never seen it before. It was big,' a boy blurts out, his eyes wide like saucers. 'Do you want me to draw it on the whiteboard?'

'Yes please,' I say.

... And we are away. Observations are heightened. This is transformational. These young writers are beginning to look at the world a little differently, their eyes and ears more focused. Possibilities are emerging in so many directions. Curious learners are in the building.

Teachers are faced with the challenge of instilling habits of mind that will hopefully last a lifetime – habits that will develop curious learners, learners infinitely fascinated and interested in the world, global citizens who persist in asking questions of themselves and others. To quote Lewis Thomas (1983), an American physician, poet, etymologist, essayist, administrator, educator, policy advisor and researcher, 'Anything wonderful is something to smile in the presence of.'

People frequently post on social media sites the painful post 'I'm bored!' seemingly in the hope the world will come to their rescue.

When discussing boredom with young learners, I find myself sharing the news that there is a miraculous cure for this common affliction. 'There's a cure,' I tell them. 'Do you want to know what it is?' Well of course they do.

'The cure for boredom is "curiosity" – and the great thing about curiosity is that once you have it, there's no known cure!'

CONSIDER

By sharing one's personal wonderment, hopefully a spark is lit. What did you see today? What did you hear today? Tell me about a conversation you overheard? Who noticed something small and wonderful today? Who was awe-struck by something they witnessed today? Be a champion for curiosity. Bring the outside in. Be a curious learner and see what you harvest from that standpoint.

3

A WRITER NEEDS TO READ

Even though I can't remember all of them, the books I love are still part of me; reading other books will remind me of them; I'll find myself quoting them in conversation or in my writing – faint memories of names and moments, all swirling, like half remembered dreams and snatches of childhood memory, to ferment, unseen in the deep delved earth of my subconscious to hopefully pop, sparkling, into my work in ways I can't yet imagine. (*'In Your Dreams', Sunil Badami, 2015*)

I love the rush that accompanies buying a new book. The browsing and rummaging that precedes the purchase. The quiet and considered contemplation as one searches the shelves in the hope of finding a reading gem. Eventually, I reach out and pluck a volume from the shelves. I relish the opportunity to turn the book over in my hands and receive the words. I scan the cover thoroughly, taking in the elements of the page before turning the book over, anticipating the blurb. If it's an author with whom I am unfamiliar, I want to get to know them. I need for us to be better acquainted; the author and me. So, I open the book to see if the dust jacket reveals information about this potential new friend. I am provided with the background information I seek. Pleased to meet you, I think...

While visiting Book and Paper, an independent bookshop in Williamstown, I chanced upon a book by John Boyne, an Irish writer and author of *The Boy in the Striped Pyjamas*. The book, titled *Noah Barleywater Runs Away*, has the word, 'runs' printed in slightly bolder text on the cover, and I wondered if this was significant. Was I meant to notice this small detail? The blurb repeated the book's opening lead. It was most engaging. A lead must draw the reader in, capture and hold their attention. It may be written in such a way as to raise questions or heighten curiosity. John Boyne aroused such a response when I read 'Noah Barleywater left home in the early morning, before the sun rose, before the dogs woke, before the dew stopped falling on the fields'.

I was struck by Boyne's deliberate efforts to deliver the reader a clear sense of time, through his effective use of repetition. I had pressing questions, such as: *Why is Noah leaving home? Where is he going?* The desire to read on, to find out, to discover, was immediately established within me as a reader. John Boyne had drawn me in. He had my attention. He had reached out with his words and grabbed my attention. He had gently shaken me to pay attention. The book left the shop under my arm.

Upon arriving home, I retrieved my notebook from my bag – such was the compelling nature of this book-buying experience. I felt a strong need to record these thoughts. There are rituals surrounding my purchasing of books. It involves quite considered actions, and because I must read with the eye of a writer, I look for titles that will deepen my knowledge and appreciation of the written word.

John Boyne's words beckon the reader in me. They support me as a writer. I need to know more.

It is frequently said that reading is the input and writing is the output. For this reason, it is important to consider carefully what we read and what we advise students to read. As Annie Dillard (1990) notes in

The Writing Life: 'The writer is careful of what he reads, for that is what he will write. He is careful of what he learns, because that is what he will know.'

Apart from learning to read widely, we must also make a point of reading what we are hoping to write. For many inexperienced writers, there continues to be a clear disconnect between what they are reading and what they wish to write. They are denying themselves opportunities to learn firsthand from authors who have written in the genre they have identified for their own writing. I often suggest to young writers that they choose two books: one they wish to read right now and a second one that will inform their writing.

Across the years, I have increasingly practised the art of reading like a writer. My notebook is a collection zone for words that offer me inspiration. Words I wish I had written. Words that make me strive to be a more effective writer. I read the words on the page, then I see them again in a clearer light. It may be a single interesting line that catches my attention. It may be intriguing word use. It may be the sound the word makes when I utter it aloud. I often feel sufficiently sparked to go in search of a word's etymology, my curiosity piqued.

I find inspiration across the entire range of my reading territories – from magazines on planes, professional readings, recreational reading, novels, newspapers, picture story books, poetry, fiction and nonfiction titles.

I have no doubt in my mind that the entries of trusted authors captured in my various notebooks have inspired my own experimentation with ideas. No doubt they have mingled with the ideas already present in my mind. The words of others have guided my own word use. These mentor authors have been influential in defining the way forward. My own experience as a writer has also played a part in shaping how I go about the task of writing. Practice and experience have allowed me to find my preferred track.

I readily acknowledge the influence of others on the writer I have become. In the beginning, we imitate. Then we innovate. I am hopefully passing on these influences in my own approach to writing.

I don't have the time or space to detail all the recorded words of fellow authors that have lit a spark in my writing mind. I have therefore chosen a representative sample. It is part of an enduring legacy. I mined my old notebooks and dug out some of the accumulated treasure. The words and advice of these authors are scattered throughout my lengthy notebook journey. They have inspired and influenced me as I have chiselled out my own particular way to live a writing kind of life.

Pearls from Assorted Pages

'The book came flapping like a wounded duck and fell at Jeffrey's feet.' *(Jerry Spinelli, Maniac Magee)*

'It resounded like a fart in a cathedral.' *(Frank Hardy, The Outcasts of Foolgarah)*

'Everything is quiet. Everything is still. It hasn't rained for two whole years.' *(Cathy Applegate and Dee Huxley, Raindance)*

'Over the hills and under the sky, the wind sent clouds the colour of bruises.' *(Helen Ward and Ian Andrews, The Boat)*

'The creature offers up another glob of blood that hits the sheet with the tiniest sound imaginable.' *(Tim Winton, Land's Edge)*

'Once I wet the toes of dinosaurs, but that was long ago. I am the ocean.' *(Suzanna Marshak, I Am the Ocean)*

'Her name was Mrs Pratchett. She was a small skinny old hag with a moustache on her upper lip and a mouth as sour as a green gooseberry.' *(Roald Dahl, Boy)*

'We crawled around the streets like the ice-cream van of the apocalypse, looking for survivors...' *(Don Watson, American Journeys)*

'His crown was dented, his castle was crumbling and the only shoes he owned were both for the left foot. He was the poorest king in all the land.' *(Kate Walker, Bogpeat Castle)*

'She had a face that looked like it was continually expecting the arrival of a bad smell.' *(John Kennedy Toole, Confederacy of Dunces)*

'Far inland, where the ocean is a dim memory, the sun floats on the waves of another bake-earth day. In the long shadows, a big red kangaroo licks his forearm and lets the early evening breeze wash over him.' *(Claire Saxby, Big Red Kangaroo)*

Advice on Writing

'Always write (and read) with the ear, not the eye. You should hear every sentence you write as if it was being read aloud.' *(C. S. Lewis, Letter to a girl named Thomasine)*

'Every lead is like a compressed draft. It reveals the subject, the writer's attitude towards the subject, the voice, the direction, the form and the order of a piece of writing.' *(Donald Murray, Making the Meaning Clear: The Logic of Revision)*

'One of the things that happens when you give yourself permission to start writing is that you start thinking like a writer. You start seeing everything as material.' *(Ann Lamott, Bird By Bird)*

'You can, you should and if you're brave enough to start, you will.' *(Stephen King, On Writing: A Memoir of the Craft)*

'Just write every day of your life and read intensely. Most of my friends who are on that diet are having very pleasant careers.' *(Ray Bradbury, Zen in the Art of Writing)*

Factoids

I have always had a fascination with facts and trivia. I love obscure information. I collect it with a relish, trapping it in my notebook just in case I can use it in some way. Here are some gems harvested from the pages of various notebooks.

The dot on top of the letter 'I' is called a tittle.

Coconuts kill more people annually than sharks.

The ball on top of the flagpole is called a truck.

The average number of licks it takes to finish an ice-cream is 50.

It is still illegal to play cards on a train in New York.

It is illegal to take a bear onto a beach in Israel.

There are ten ways to be dismissed in the game of cricket.

Chickens outnumber human beings 4:1.

It is illegal to lock your car doors in Manitoba, Canada, in case someone needs to seek shelter from a polar bear.

In Texas, it is illegal to put graffiti on someone else's cow.

99 per cent of people cannot lick their elbow.

Polar bears weigh only 600 grams when born.

More than 12 million people in the world make a living fishing from boats.

Pigs can't look up at the sky.

Australia is wider than the moon.

The Spanish national anthem has no words.

Most Important Thoughts

Sometimes a single word can spark a host of writing possibilities. On one occasion I began thinking about the word 'most'. I began posing questions to myself. Questions involving 'mosts'. From there, a series of personal 'mosts' began to form in my mind. I find myself indulging in this sort of inquiry quite frequently, I must admit…

- *The most people I have seen gathered in one place…*
  Well, that was in New York City when I proudly took part in a peace march against the Iraq War. Almost 200,000 people participated that day (in 2003) in what was a large-scale peaceful statement of collective concern about the invasion of Iraq.

- *The most daring thing I've done so far…*
  White-water rafting on the Barron River in Cairns, Queensland. Closely followed by jumping into a swimming pool in the depths of winter in my younger days just to win a bet.

- *The most rain I ever saw…*
  Innisfail, Queensland, 1989. I was holidaying there and it rained for 14 out of 16 days I was there. Wet, wet, wet. Moist and mouldy air.

- *The most trouble I ever got into as a child…*
  That was surely the time my dad noticed my singed eyebrows and smelled the smoke on my clothes before asking me directly if I had been smoking. Without hesitating, I told him, 'No, I was only lighting them for the other kids.' My father was more disappointed by the fact that I had so blatantly lied, than the fact that I had experimented with the dreaded scourge of cigarettes. Ironically, my father smoked for almost 30 years, while I never wanted to take it up. Maybe that humiliating experience aged nine was enough to put me off for life.

We all have our personal 'mosts'. It's a close relative of 'firsts'. Once you tap into the idea, it can reveal a rich vein of potential ideas. I'll stop there for now. You can imagine that there are many more 'most' moments should I need them.

Why Writers Collect Words They Admire

Writers need to read extensively. They often read a wide variety of things and are frequently drawn to words and ideas written in particular genres, styles and forms, according to their individual interests and writing projects. Writers frequently collect different kinds of writing. Why?

They harvest these extracts, quotes, words and works for amusement, inspiration, curiosity and fascination. Writers often closely study such pieces in order to develop their own writing, their own technique and ideas.

The point I'm making here is that it is quite legitimate to collect such words in your own writer's notebook. By doing this, you allow yourself and your words to be guided and inspired by writers you admire. Hopefully the words nestling beside your words encourage you to strive to emulate your writing mentors. For many young writers, the thought of collecting examples from writers they admire might never have crossed their minds. This knowledge is valuable. It's a licence to explore, to learn from literary heroes.

Writers collect writing they find appealing. Once collected, that piece of writing can be read and reread for enjoyment and inspiration. It also enables the writer to learn more about particular writing styles and topics and craft strategies.

Inexperienced writers should be encouraged to add such items to their writers' notebooks. Asking them why a writer might choose a particular piece of writing and what that reveals about their interest becomes a critical question. Every so often, allow time for the mindful sharing of some of the writing that has been curated. In the discussion, seek to discover why they chose to harvest particular entries. Encourage young writers to name the title and author they are referencing and how that author may have influenced their writing.

It is important to allow students to brainstorm and discuss how they might explore ways of collecting writing samples that appeal to them, samples they find inspirational. They can be alerted to the fact that such actions allow them to stimulate their own writing by tapping into the creative talent of more experienced writers. Further note how experienced writers often mention authors or books that have influenced their work as writers.

As teacher/writer, you can look at examples you have collected in your own notebook – quotes, extracts, articles, poems, cartoons. Share them and elaborate on their significance. Why did you consider them worthy of retention in your notebook? Have you learned something from these entries? Have they influenced something you have written?

Possible Writer Actions

- Collect writing samples you like – books, articles, reviews, poems, quotes, extracts, short stories, song lyrics. Use them to reference ideas and craft strategies you might like to try.
- Collect strong leads, beginnings, introductions.
- Collect interesting endings.
- Collect interesting and unusual words.
- Collect strong character descriptions.
- Collect great descriptions of scenes and settings.
- Collect powerful dialogue.
- Collect examples of 'show, don't tell'.
- Collect examples of 'mood' and 'tone'.
- Collect examples of literary elements like simile, metaphor, alliteration, onomatopoeia.
- Collect examples of the powerful use of verbs, nouns, adjectives.
- Collect poems.
- Collect quotes, extracts.
- Collect news and magazine articles.
- Collect cartoons.
- Collect song lyrics.
- Collect reviews.
- Collect jokes, riddles, short stories.
- Collect noteworthy letters.

CONSIDER

Each and every time we enter a classroom to teach writing, we must bring with us all the reading and writing we have ever done. These authors are our unwitting collaborators. We are lifted on the wings of our heroes.

There is much to be gained from spending time in bookshops. It sustains our literary mindset. It holds the potential to challenge and invigorate our thinking. We have the opportunity to be alerted about possibilities. The bookshop exists as an essential connection. It is a place to make discoveries, discoveries we are able to share willingly and enthusiastically with fellow literary souls. Time spent among the words of other authors keeps us healthy. It helps to know we are never alone as writers. I make it a habit to visit bookshops on a regular basis. That's where the gold is buried.

4

EMBRACING INSPIRATION

I frequently take a suitcase with me when I visit schools. I look like I am going on vacation and I've overshot the airport. My suitcase is invariably filled with books: favourite books, mentor texts, collected writers' notebooks, newly acquired books. I call it my *suitcase of surprises*. When I enter a classroom, the assembled students peer forward, hoping to gain an advanced sighting of the contents. A sneak-peek.

On one occasion I brought a collection of writers' notebooks to share. During my previous visit, I had informed the class I would be bringing them. They had gathered some artefacts and made some preliminary lists of things they considered potential topics for their writing. Neither the teacher nor the students had much previous experience with using writers' notebooks. They quickly formed into groups of three and I distributed the notebooks. 'I want you to be readers and researchers. I want you to be text detectives and make a note of the different types of entries you see in these notebooks.'

I wanted them to see the broad influences on my writing. 'You will learn about the writer and what catches the writer's eye. You will learn the writer's preferences and personal history,' I added. I made it clear that no two notebooks are exactly alike and the way I have shaped my notebooks is just one way to collect your writing ideas. It is not the only way. They scanned the notebook pages, asking questions, seeking clarification regarding entries:

'Have you been to Turkey?'

'Why have you drawn a map of your nana's house?'

'How come you have business cards in your notebook?'

'Where did you get the idea for that poem?'

'Did you really set an emu on fire?'

'Is that you?'

'What are cicadas?'

'Did that really happen?'

All valid questions. Lists were compiled regarding the variety of entries each group of researchers found. The information noted was then shared with other groups and the knowledge pooled. The students were invited to create a list in their own notebooks as a reminder of the kinds of entries they might like to gather in the coming days and weeks. It would become a framework for their future collecting as observers.

They made lists of the entry types they found. The information they noted was then shared with other groups and the knowledge pooled. Knowledge floats on a sea of talk and talk filled the classroom.

The lists included such things as:

- News headlines
- Reports
- Letters
- Cards
- Reviews
- Questions

- Artefacts/keepsakes
- Persuasive pieces
- Jokes
- Pictures
- News articles
- Tickets
- Recounts
- Memoir pieces
- Narratives
- Nonfiction
- Fiction
- Extracts
- Quotes
- Lists
- Maps
- Drawings
- Poems
- Stories
- Business cards
- Brochures
- Photographs

'More than anything, what did you notice about my notebook entries?' I then enquired.

'Lots of writing. So much writing.'

'You're absolutely correct. It's a writer's notebook. Writers have to write.'

I returned to the same classroom two weeks later to see what progress these young writers had made with their notebook entries.

What a pleasant surprise! Upon entering the room, notebooks were thrust at me. 'Hey, Alan, look at what I have done.' Lists, poems, longer entries, opinion pieces, photographs with captions, drawings, plans, and assorted artefacts were all captured and presented. These developing writers were proud of their efforts. The pieces I read were varied and interesting. The energy around writing was palpable. I could not wait to share my uplifting experience with the principal and further validate the great things happening here. Good news deserves to be shared. They say feeling smart about something generates energy. It was clearly on display here. Obvious pride poured out of these young writers as they shared an array of entries. 'I've got two notebooks now. One for school and one for home,' beamed one enthusiastic writer.

Letting students see how a fellow writer – a more experienced writer – goes about harvesting writing ideas and feeding their writing life had worked its special magic.

The teacher also had a story to share concerning notebooks. Held proudly in hand, the teacher's own writer's notebook was presented. The writer within was re-emerging. The notebook pages were filling. A strong light was beginning to shine within this classroom community. A new challenge presents itself at this point: how do we sustain the energy that has been unleashed?

I have observed many teachers sharing entries from their writers' notebooks with students. They read their entries, explaining to the eager young writers seated before them the inspiration behind the writing. They talk of connections and speculate on future entries. They discuss how they overcame problems arising from the writing being shared. They display the pages of their notebooks and point out various pictures and artefacts. The pleasure derived from the writing experiences of the teachers is most apparent. This is powerful modelling. When writing teachers choose to operate in this way, an expectation is set for students to follow. It is bold teaching. Learning to write becomes a shared journey for teachers and students alike. The genesis of a writing community is established by such actions. All participants are connected to the same challenge: the challenge to write.

As the school year unfolds, the writing begins to move beyond the four walls of the classroom. Encouraged by their teachers, students begin taking their notebooks home and finding a host of places to gather writing inspiration. They develop preferences, choosing where to write and when to write. They adopt the behaviours of more experienced writers. Under these conditions, writing moves beyond something that you do for a teacher. There is a sense of genuine ownership here. The writer's notebook becomes a travelling companion as well as a writing resource.

Writers, Start Your Engines!

Childhood is a rich source of writing inspiration for all writers. For a teacher unaccustomed to writing with their students, it is a great place to begin.

It is that place and time in our lives when curiosity and experience collided and sparks flew. Curiosity was at its peak and experience was in short supply during childhood. It is where we all discovered consequences, painful lessons, joy and success, emotional legacies and the reality of our physical limitations. It is in childhood that we first don the cape of invincibility, only to be left holding a somewhat tattered remnant as we enter adulthood.

As a starting point for writing, I encourage inexperienced adult writers to recall aspects of childhood. The range of experience is usually quite vast, ranging from disappointment to triumph! The full range of human emotions is on display here, condensed into this brief, yet special, time of our lives.

Starting in this place will assist a teacher new to writing to connect strongly with the lives of their students. It will enable the teacher writer to convey the importance of capturing those small, yet significant moments in our lives. Being the most experienced writer in the room enables a teacher to readily employ the senses to enliven the writing.

We reveal our humanity when we write about our childhoods. Childhood is a treasure chest waiting to be opened. The voices that emerge will be different, of course; some will tell of loss and disappointment, and others will tell of dreams realised and heartfelt memories. However, if the words are honest, the writing will be of interest to the eager young audience.

Words are capable of crossing time and space. The adult writer can forge a connection with a younger generation through stories that tell of a similar age and experience. Amy Ehrlich (1996), writing in *When I Was Your Age*, portrays childhood stories in this way: 'These are special places yet ordinary; taken for granted at the time but etched and glowing in memory. Quite simply, they are home.'

CONSIDER

Should you choose to take up the challenge of writing about your childhood, try to avoid the overlay of adult perspective in the early throes of these memoir pieces. Consider the age of the audience. It might prove more valuable to write from the persona of your inner child. Place yourself in the time the event originally took place. What you need is a time machine mentality that enables you to whizz back in time for a moment.

Now consider the following perspectives:

- Your size in relation to the world surrounding you at the time the event took place. The world shrinks as we grow up.
- Your knowledge or lack of it regarding the world and how it operates. We learn through experience that not all dogs and people are friendly, you can't jump over every puddle, and sadness fades with time.
- Your feelings towards the various protagonists in your writing pieces –parents, siblings, friends, perceived enemies and the rest. We all remember the catch cry 'It's not fair!'
- Your level of power in relation to the events that took place. It was a time when giants ruled your world, remember.
- The discrepancy between what you think happened and the reality of the situation. Memories are our version of the truth.

You may choose to write a follow-up paragraph from a grown-up perspective and outline any effect the experience may have had for you – any lingering reminders, or the lessons learned. Remember, it's just one way into the writing that students are grappling with each and every day. Think of your stories as Velcro, connecting you to the work of a group of developing writers.

5

THE POWER OF WORDS

Language tells us who we are: because we are the words we use. If we adopt the language of another society, we lose our rights to memory in our own kingdom.

These words belong to social anthropologist Hugh Lunn (2006), from his book *Lost for Words*. Lunn is fearful that we are in danger of losing our respective language identities – that language is becoming increasingly homogenised and simplified.

We know from experience that language is ever changing and evolving. That excites me. New words are constantly entering the lexicon. Social media now plays a role in spreading those words. Words are being spread at an ever-increasing speed: globalised language. However, at the other end we appear to be losing one heck of a lot of rich and expressive language. Television 'speak' has stunted our range of language terms. Shades of meaning have been reduced. Many people are now content to use a few stock phrases to get by. They figure it saves time, I guess. These stock phrases have replaced a plethora of words and sayings that were once a feature of conversation. You hear people fill conversations with colourless grabs. Expressions such as *whatever, tell someone who cares, get over it* or *get a life* have become universal. Our conversational language has become simple and standardised, like corporate standardisation in the fast-food industry. Just listen to the way the word 'like' is sprinkled through conversation on the street, in cafés, at schools, on television. 'I was like waiting for the bus, when this guy like rode his bike into the bus shelter. I was like, oh my God, like totally amazed.' It grates on the ear. It stands as a monument to intellectual laziness.

The rich and colourful terminology once spoken has been replaced by evasive, nondescript utterings. You still hear rich phrases used in conversation, but they appear slightly endangered, having fallen from favour. They have become language relics – a bit like the people who use them.

Let me explain what I mean. My mother gave me great advice over the years. The best of it usually came during those times when I was catastrophising – love that word. I would be working myself into a lather and she might offer such rich gems as:

- No use crying over split milk.
- These things are sent to try us.
- Never mind, you'll survive.
- Let's cross that bridge when we come to it.
- We'll just have to make do with what we have.
- We'll just have to start again, won't we?

Today I am more likely to hear the simple generic utterance 'Get a life'.

It is apparent that expressions have become inhibited. I find myself using terms and phrases from my childhood that draw blank expressions from generations that have somehow missed out on this amazingly rich lexicon. Today words such as 'like', 'nasty' and 'puh-lease' act as conversational glue. Expressions such as 'Bring it on', 'Oh my God' and 'In your dreams' are heard ad nauseum. This style of talk is abbreviated, dismissive and all too common. The idiom has suffered at the hands of modern culture and television's dumbing-down effects.

Overheard

Over the years I have honed my eavesdropping abilities. I listen actively to the sounds around me. I have made a point of collecting expressions such as the following in my notebooks:

- 'My mother-in-law has a look that could burn holes in the lawn.'
- 'I feel as welcome as a skunk at a garden party.'
- 'Stop your gum thumping!'
- 'You're more likely to be kicked by a snake.'
- 'That's okay, you can be the designated basket-case.'
- 'He's got all the direction of a blowfly in a bottle!'
- 'He couldn't hit the side of a barn with a bagful of wheat!'
- 'You can't make strawberry jam out of cow manure.'
- 'That's better than getting a slater up your nose.'

It is not merely nostalgia that makes me long for this rich and colourful use of language. I am concerned that future generations may miss out on this expressive language as we increasingly adopt a generic kind of communication. We'll no longer value such wonderful terms as *dunderhead, dingbat, nong* and *ninny*. People will stare in utter disbelief when I describe someone as being 'a few sandwiches short of a picnic'. I know I'll be down in the dumps and feeling as miserable as a bandicoot when that happens. Forgive my bellyaching, I'm just being a grizzleguts and, like Hugh Lunn, I too am lost for words. As writers, we are charged with the responsibility to record language for posterity. My attention to words and phrases, dialect and idiom is bound up in this quest.

If I didn't indulge in a little eavesdropping, I would miss out on the kind of magic present in the following snatches of conversation gently nestled in my notebooks for consideration at some later time:

Monica read her writing piece to me. It began, 'I walked into the kitchen and Mum's head was on the table.' She suddenly stopped, looked at me and added, 'That sounds all wrong, doesn't it?' I smiled and nodded my head in agreement, unless she was writing a horror story that I didn't know about.

A student seated at the back of the group raised his hand enthusiastically, looked me directly in the eye and told me, 'We did lots of brain-draining.'

'Close,' I said. 'I think you mean brainstorming, although sometimes it does feel a little draining.'

… Ah yes, from the innocent we often get refreshing honesty and accuracy.

The mind of a small child is both curious and unique in its appreciation of the world. A pre-school child of a friend encountered a spider and asked, 'What's that?'

The parent replied, 'It's a daddy long legs.'

The child paused briefly before asking, 'Where's the mummy long legs?'

'He had the voice of an angel and the body of a dugong.' A comment overheard on the radio.

I regularly gather conversation gold while seated quietly in cafés:

> 'What's he do?'
> 'He's an investmentologist.'
> 'A what?'
> 'I don't really know, to be honest.'

> 'How are you, Pam?'
> 'It's Jan, not Pam.'
> 'Jan?'
> 'Yes, Jan.'
> 'Oh, sorry, Jan, I thought you were Pam.'

On one occasion, while waiting for my x-ray appointment at the hospital, a young woman walks by and immediately informs a passing nurse, 'I'm looking for my nana.'

'Okay, what's her name?' asks the nurse.

'NANA,' replies the young woman, seemingly surprised the nurse is unaware of the person to whom she refers.

I struck up a conversation with a security guard at a school in Brooklyn, New York, and he informed me, 'I have trouble with little creatures like centipedes. Can you believe the Army trained me to kill people?'

Two women sat on a wooden bench outside the shopping precinct. Both of them were smoking and looking like they were sitting in the naughty corner. One woman drew hard on her cigarette, exhaled slowly towards the sky before jabbing a finger towards her friend. 'As soon as money were mentioned, she were there, she were there. She were there like a cannonball,' she snapped. Her mouth moved vigorously, as if she was chewing on a wasp sandwich.

It's Only Words and Words Are All I Have...

I have always had a fascination for words. Words deserve our respect. Writers collect words. It is compulsive and totally necessary. If we can get the right word in the right place, we give the reader a nudge and make them pay extra attention. Words matter.

I am unashamedly a word collector. I am a proud logophile. I listen to the sounds words make. When they are spoken, it is an auraculous experience – a wonder of the ear. I admire their shape. I say them out loud. I record them in my notebooks and constantly look for the right opportunity to insert them into my writing. I recall as a child frequently delving into dictionaries in search of new words. My notebooks are repositories for all kinds of word gathering – strange and mysterious words, exotic words, newly invented words sit alongside colloquial terms. I feel compelled to harvest words.

When these pearls bob up in conversation, or on the page, or reveal themselves in floating dialogue, I collect them with relish. It's like finding treasure washed up on the beach. I am bedazzled.

I vividly recall reading Colin Thiele's (1974) wonderful short story 'The Lock-Out' to a Grade 6 class quite some years back and coming across the words *agog* and *gingerly*. I wrote them on the board, and we discussed them and savoured the sounds they made. I encouraged the students to try and use these gems in their writing. In time these words, along with others we had noted and discussed, began to emerge in the students' writing. They grew like flowers – blossoming on the page, magically bursting through into the light. We developed a place for those special words we came across in our reading and discussion. We called them 'wonder words'. It was a way of paying homage to the richness and meaning such words conveyed.

Sometimes I recall or hear a word or phrase that has fallen out of use and I attempt to revive it by sprinkling it into my conversations. I find beauty in old words. Words rarely used. Words from English and other languages that ring in my ears and beg to be slotted into conversations. I am grateful to Robert Macfarlane (2015) and his wonderful book *Landmarks* for introducing me to a host of beautiful old words that owe their existence to the landscapes of my ancestors in Britain and Ireland. Robert is a fine writer and a word warrior. He defends and exults words – ancient and unusual. Words like *smirr* (soft, mist-like precipitation), *fizmer* (a rustling noise produced in grass by gentle wind agitation), *scraunching* (vegetation withering with the heat) or *spangin* (to walk vigorously).

I recently came across the word *skedaddle* (after many years) in Helga Bansch's (2011) picture story book *Odd Bird Out*, a story about a non-conformist raven. The text is rich in its word use, with a liberal sprinkling of idiomatic language. *Skedaddle* is a word I recall from my childhood, but I had neither seen nor heard it for *yonks* (an indeterminate yet substantial period of time). I love the sound of *skedaddle*. I have been sharing it with young writers recently in the hope I can singlehandedly revive its use in common conversation. As kids, we frequently *skedaddled* from the scene, particularly when something *nefarious* had happened. I also loved words like *scallywag, whippersnapper* and *rascal* and how those words were ascribed to us when we were kids. It was a badge of honour to be labelled that way.

I had a thing about the word *piffle* a while back. So much so, I felt compelled to write a poem about it. That's how compulsive my word collecting has become. I love the word *hullabaloo*. It's a word that makes me ponder. Just how loud is a *hullabaloo*? Is it louder than a *commotion*? It sounds louder than a *kerfuffle* or a *ruckus*, to me anyway. Then there is that wonderful word *squabble*. *Squabble* rhymes with wobble and suggests disquiet and disruption. 'They're having a bit of a *squabble*, it seems.'

I often wonder where such words began. For instance, the word *clodhopper* is used when referring to someone who is wearing unusually large shoes or boots. The word clod makes me think of clods of dirt, so I tend to think of *clodhopper* as having rural origins. Boots big enough to step over clods of dirt. I am a person who wears big *clodhoppers*. As a boy, my father frequently reminded me: 'Watch where you put your big *clodhoppers*!'

I am curious about *spurious*. It has a sound to it that appeals. *Spurious claims* sound so much better than *false claims*. Spurious possesses a certain power.

I love the Italian word *segue*. I love the sound of it, but I also love that it is spelt in such a unique way. It is common in conversation but largely unseen in print. If you don't believe me, ask people to spell it and see what happens. They say a difficult word is a word we have rarely sighted. I also love the sound of French words like *boulevard, au fait* and *aperitif*. They're fun to *smatter* through a conversation.

I came across the word *calamitous* while randomly browsing through Annie Dillard's (1974) *Pilgrim at Tinker Creek* in search of some words I wish I'd written. I immediately felt the need to use it – surround it with words of my own. I found myself gathering words and ideas for a piece about nearby Fisherman's Beach and so I added this sentence to my notebook entries: 'The piercing squeals of children chasing each other reverberated along the beach. Armed with clumps of seaweed they streaked about with *calamitous* wailing.'

Words have an *allure*, a charm. They are the wonderful creation of the *exquisite* and seemingly infinite use of those magical 26 letters we have at our disposal.

If I look toward the bookshelves in my study, a number of titles on display further reinforce the view that words are important to me. Titles such as *The Word Spy*, *Lost for Words*, *The Superior Person's Little Book of Words*, *The Boy Who Loved Words*, along with assorted dictionaries designed for writers, poets and those obsessed with rhyme, stand as testimony to my ongoing love of words.

The great thing about words is that they are constantly being invented. A new word enters the lexicon on average every 98 minutes. Sadly, words also fall out of use. Sometimes those words are well worth reviving. A writer needs words just as a fish needs water.

In Charlotte Zolotow's evocative *The Seashore Book*, first published in 1992, the author sets the scene for a child's day of discovery at the beach with his mother. At one point she describes the scene when mother and son are seated on the rocks eating sandwiches and drinking lemonade as they watch 'the small brown sand-crabs squaggling at our toes'. That word *squaggling* demands my attention. I am unable to resist it. I trap it in my notebook. It's the kind of word that attracts a red line when I later type it into my computer. I love it.

I recall how my science and biology teacher, Tony Phillips, in his frustration often referred to distractible students as 'confounded nincompoops'. While my octogenarian neighbour Margaret had a fondness for the word 'charlatan', which she frequently abbreviated to 'char'. Any slightly dodgy or dubious character was referred to as a char.

This search for wondrous words knows no end. They seep into my published work. Words such as:

- Scallywag
- Vamoosed
- Syncopation
- Dooverlackie
- Viscous
- Macaroon
- Plummet
- Goop.

Then there are words waiting in the wings for a call-up:

- Mingy
- Wallop
- Finicky
- Hunky-dory
- Frizzled
- Discombobulated.

In his book *Pyrotechnics on the Page*, Ralph Fletcher (2010) provided a timely reminder of the importance of active listening when he stated, 'We write with the ear as much as with the eye or the mind.' I was unconsciously attending to this aspect of writing, but Ralph's articulation of this important fact allowed me to be more consciously skilled. When we write with our ears, we become aware of the sound of language, the rhyme and rhythm of language and the impact of words uttered. We are more likely to connect the words that float our way to our prior knowledge. We are more likely to retain these words in our conscious memory. We are more likely to record and reuse them.

When we purposefully attend to the sounds that surround us and the sound of words as we read, we add an extra dimension to our lives as writers. Becoming aware of this fact allows the teaching of writing to shift from the *what* (subject/meaning/content) to the *how* (language). This is where writing comes to life. This is where reading like a writer finds its origins.

Occasionally I launch into a workshop by playing a song. I ask participants to attend to the lyrics. I direct their attention to those words and phrases that stand out for them. Those word threads that command their attention – and demand to be held in the mind of the listener. I ask them to write down the selected words and to think about any possible connections. *Why these words? What is their power? What is their significance to you as a listener?*

On one occasion, I selected Canadian singer/songwriter Bruce Cockburn's song 'Last Night of the World'. For me, Cockburn's rich lyrics were perfect for this type of activity. He is a keen observer, and his writing possesses a strong poetic thread. And at the end of the day, I really like the song.

The audience listened intently and quietly made notes. At the song's end, I invited everyone to *turn and talk* about their notations. The room instantly filled with rich conversations. Many made strong connections, often based on a single word. It was a powerful reminder of the power of active and conscious listening. I wished we had been able to explore this more extensively. If time had permitted, I could have challenged them to each 'lift a line' and use it to generate a piece of writing.

I explained to the gathering how my own writing life relies on eavesdropping to gather so many ideas. I gather snatches of conversation and listen to the wondrous and infinite combinations of spoken words. The structure of language informs each of us as writers – its patterns, its quirks. The workshop continued. The point had been made. Friends, Romans and anyone else listening right now, let's hear it for ears!

I'll leave it there. You get the picture. Right now, though, I need to *skedaddle…*

May I Quote You on That?

A teacher asked if she could take a peek inside my writer's notebook. I agreed. I am always prepared to share. After all, that's what writers do. A peek is but a small thing to ask.

When she handed it back to me, she thanked me for sharing, and then commented on some of the quotes she had noted while scanning the pages. 'Where did you find these quotes?' She asked.

I informed her that I source them everywhere I go. Some of them I hear, many of them I read on my regular reading journeys through books, the internet, Twitter and Facebook.

As we talked, I began to consider why I gather such material. As writers, we are gatherers and collectors. I believe I harvest these words because they inspire me to greater efforts. I harvest them because they remind me of my responsibilities as an educator. Some of them are just plain funny, and I embrace the opportunity to have a good laugh. Some quotes are collected because they contain vital messages I can share with others. Occasionally I aim to apply them to writing pieces to support the thrust of my work. Sometimes I need the words as sustenance for the soul. At other times, they serve as reminders that I can always improve as a human being. So, I am grateful to this teacher, for she enabled me to reflect upon an aspect of my practice as both a writer and an educator.

Here are some examples of recent quotations from the pages of my notebooks:

> 'Never use a metaphor, simile or other figure of speech which you are used to seeing in print.' *(George Orwell, Politics and the English Language)*

> 'Life is short, make sure you are wearing your happy pants.' *(A woman being interviewed on television)*

> 'Writing becomes reading and reading is the finest teacher of how to write.' *(Annie Proulx, Annie Proulx on Language, Writing and More)*

> 'I can't write without a reader. It's precisely like a kiss – you can't do it alone.' *(John Cheever, The Journals of John Cheever)*

> 'Don't put your fingers in your mouth when you're pushing a supermarket trolley.' *(Neil Finn, Twitter post)*

> 'Writers end up writing about their obsessions. Things that haunt them; things they can't forget; stories they carry in their bodies.' *(Alex Myers, Supporting Transgender Students)*

The Wonder of Wordplay

Wordplay is such an omnipotent thing. It is unavoidable. Conversation, songs, TV shows, advertisements, literature, greeting cards, brochures, magazines and newspapers all employ wordplay abundantly. Everywhere we go, it leaps out at us.

As a person who writes, wordplay amounts to gymnastics for the mind. It entertains me. It presents a challenge I willingly embrace. It involves the critical rehearsal, so important to a writer. When I am indulging in wordplay, a smile emerges before the words have the chance to spill out and across the pages of my notebook. The notebook becomes a playground.

In many schools, however, the study of words has, over time, diminished in size to mean little more than reading and vocabulary knowledge. We have lost so much of the playfulness of words and the knowledge surrounding their use. Yet, I recall my teachers encouraging me to play with malapropisms and oxymorons, listen for tautology and wonder at the mystery of invented words in Lewis Carroll's poem 'Jabberwocky'. I recall the fun we had creating rhyming couplets and discovering palindromic words. We experimented with rhyming slang and pig-Latin.

At home, my father regularly engaged me in wordplay and riddles. There was also a fair smattering of what are now termed 'Dad jokes'. A lot of it stuck. To this day, wordplay continues to entertain me and provoke my thinking.

Why is Wordplay Important?

Well, for a start it's motivating, and from an educative perspective, it remains central to a word-rich classroom. Further to this, it requires a fair degree of word rehearsal, and this encourages the growth of meta-cognitive reflection on words. This is essential for developing writers.

Wordplay can inform the work of writers when they allow themselves to be influenced by riddles, jokes, puns, songs and poems and begin to experiment with words and use them in new ways. As with any new skill, to become embedded in practice, consistent and deliberate practice is essential. I allow myself this sweet indulgence of conscious playfulness with words frequently. This takes place in the safe knowledge that, once a writer gains knowledge of the rules governing language, they know how to break those same rules. Now, that's when the fun begins.

My writer's notebook is where these subversive activities are undertaken. I can:

- Hang out with words – old, new and invented
- Sharpen my unique identity as a writer
- Engage in playing around with language
- Use language explicitly and mindfully
- Dare to surprise
- Collect inspiring examples of wordplay from books, newspapers, magazines
- Model my own playful writing.

I have noted over many years how prevalent wordplay is in my notebooks. Multiple examples exist where words are collected, applied, invented and enjoyed. Wordplay has informed a lot of my writing, particularly my writing of poetry.

Why Engage In Wordplay? That's simple. It's fun.

Fun leads to ownership, engagement and flow. For many writers, fun matters a great deal. I count myself among such writers. We MUST encourage young writers to explore the possibilities of wordplay. It possesses the potential to elevate their writing, above the ordinary. This is a noble pursuit.

> There's no reason to believe there's a perfect word waiting for every storytelling need. When the occasion arises and the

right word isn't in the dictionary, make one up. We custom make suits and chilli and tricked out cars – so why not words? *(Jerry Spinelli, Interview)*

We do think in words and the fewer words we know, the more restricted our thoughts. As our vocabulary expands, so does our power to think. *(Madeleine L'Engle, A Circle of Quiet)*

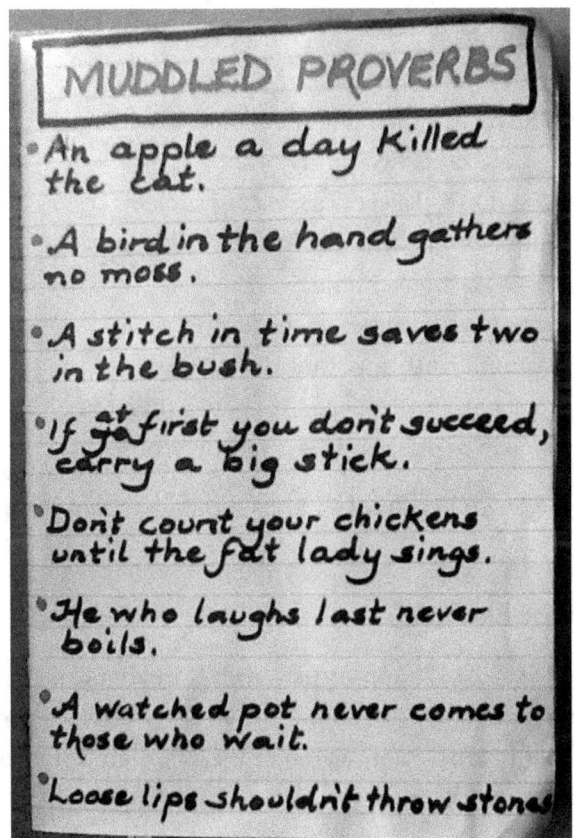

Wordplay informs my writing of poetry... Those muddled proverbs eventually found their way into one of my poems.

Muddled Messages

I'll give you some advice,
And I'll give it for free.
You'd be a fool to listen to me.
I gathered some wisdom.
I'll share it with you.
A little bit muddled,
But it's the best I can do.
In November, always remember:
An apple a day killed the cat.
A bird in the hand gathers no moss.
A stitch in time saves two in the bush.
If at first you don't succeed, carry a big stick.
Don't count your chickens until the fat lady sings.
He who laughs last never boils.
A watched pot never comes to those who wait.
Loose lips shouldn't throw stones.
While the cat's away, two heads are better than one.
People who live in glass houses spoil the broth.

Alan j Wright (from 'I Bet There's No Broccoli on the Moon')

Today I am Listing...

I love making lists. Not shopping lists, mind you, but lists that stimulate my ideas for writing. My notebooks are dotted with lists. I rummaged through my old notebooks in search of them. I share some examples of lists I found:

- Things that are slow
- Things the world doesn't need
- Things that really upset me
- Things I have done only once
- Things I love about Vicki
- Facts about my life that involve figures
- A bucket list of things that will never happen for me

- Smells I can't abide
- Things I wish I could do
- Simple, heavenly things
- Things I will never buy
- Things Dad says when he's angry
- Things parents have had enough of.

For me, lists are fun. The thinking and composing of lists are a great way to get the creative juices flowing. I enjoy the challenge of brainstorming and the thought that unexpected treasure might be unearthed. Lists represent the raw stuff from which writing may grow.

My Summer Memories

The memories of summers long ago are aroused by the writing of others.

- Swallowing flies
- Calomine lotion on sunburn
- The sound of crickets at dusk
- Playing games of 'Monoply' that lasted all week
- Performing concerts for our families
- Playing 'release' after dinner until our parents called us in or the mosquitoes got to us
- Playing backyard cricket with my sister Jeanette after dinner. She would bat and I would bowl my 'googlies' at her using the leather case. In the gathering evening gloom, she would wince as the ball connected with her leg, arm, shoulder and on occasions the bat.
- A lawn of dandelion flowers.

On one occasion I found myself thinking about a list of things I have never done that I assumed others had. This idea came from watching the Graham Norton Show, where the host asked audience members to share some of their 'never' moments.

This is what eventually appeared in my notebook:

> *Things I Have Never Done That I Assume Others Have:*
>
> I have never seen the movie *Avatar*.
>
> I have never eaten tuna.
>
> I have never read a Harry Potter book.
>
> I have never attended the Australian Formula One Grand Prix in Melbourne.
>
> I have never attended the Australian Open Tennis at Rod Laver Arena.
>
> I have never attended a yoga session.
>
> I have never watched 'Master Chef'.
>
> I have never worn a tuxedo.
>
> I have never been on a cruise.
>
> I have never eaten a Krispy Kreme doughnut.
>
> I have never believed in an afterlife.
>
> I have never broken a bone in my body.
>
> I have never had a tattoo.
>
> I have never been for a ride on a Ferris wheel.

You get the idea…

Lists help the writer organise thoughts. Lists alleviate that sense of sometimes feeling overwhelmed. They also help the writer recall details and events that can be used to inform future writing pieces. They present a host of potential writing ideas.

I sometimes use a listing strategy called 10-10-1, which goes like this:

- Make a list of at least ten items.
- Choose one item from the list and create a new list of ten things related to that original item.
- Choose one item from the second list to write about in detail.

This is a great way to narrow down the focus of the writing piece.

CONSIDER

Lists hold so much potential. Each item has the potential to be a writing topic. Lists can be used to analyse options and choices for writing. They make it easy to manage information. You can use lists to collect the things you need. They activate our prior knowledge around a topic or theme. You begin to hunt and gather things in preparation for further writing. Such stimulation!

Once you have a list, you can sort, rank and rate the items on your list. This can help you focus your attention on the things that count for you as a writer. However, when creating a list, it is quantity before quality. Just list the items as they come to you. The sorting out comes later. Don't censor in your head. You'll end up with a stilted list if you do this.

6

THE EFFECTS OF DISTANCE...

If you've never stared off into the distance, then your life is a shame. ('Mrs Potter's Lullaby', Counting Crows)

In my final year of high school, I travelled to Central Australia with my teachers and classmates and in that vast remote space experienced the night sky in a manner I could never have imagined.

One evening, in the middle of the Simpson Desert, we were camped adjacent to an artesian waterhole situated on a gibber plain. 'Gibber' is an aboriginal word loosely translating to 'stones able to be picked up in the hand and thrown', so the surrounding landscape was a carpet of small stones stretching to the horizon. In that isolated location, so removed from the city, the night sky put on a display forever etched in my memory bank. The stars shone with an intensity I had never previously experienced. A star garden of luminous quality greeted our collective eyes as we stood gazing into the night sky. The moon and the stars illuminated the gibber plain, transforming it into an illusionary world of snow. A trick of the light? Absolutely! But mesmerisingly beautiful at the same time.

Here we were, in the middle of an immense island continent, a world away from civilisation and its associated pollutants and man-made illuminations, witnessing a night sky of clear and unadulterated intensity. A collective wow echoed out across the desert darkness. The distance had provided a rare opportunity to view the stars in a way city dwellers could never easily comprehend. The distance between this place and civilisation had enabled an unparalleled view of the stars. A view of the heavens few appreciate. This was how the ancients witnessed the stars.

This was special. We were staring at superstars in every true sense. I understand what it means to be a star gazer. This experience brought into sharp perspective the benefit of distance. As the saying goes, you had to be there…

Over the last decade, I have travelled extensively in my work as well as for relaxation. Such journeys have chipped away at my worldly ignorance. I have visited many different world locations and been provided with insights and adventures. My thirst to explore and learn more remains unquenched. However, as much as I love these privileged opportunities, I am always grateful to return home – to touch base with my regular surroundings. My heart remains anchored in the place I call home. It is the distances I travel that add to my appreciation of my special place on the planet. I hanker for my precious patch. Going away makes coming home an extra reward for undertaking the journey. The distance I create between my temporary location and my heart's home serves to reinforce its importance. The familiar is viewed with fresh appreciation. I cease to take it for granted. I view the place I call home with a keener eye. It is a place in my heart, after all.

During the six years I lived in New York, I visited the famous Metropolitan Museum of Art on numerous occasions. On one such visit I found myself standing directly in front of Vincent van Gogh's 'Irises'. This painting was one of a series. It depicts irises in a vase with a pink background. With time, the pink had faded to an off-white. The size of the painting struck me immediately. It was much smaller than I had imagined. I initially viewed Van Gogh's work at close range. However, it was when I stepped back a little that I fully appreciated the beauty the painter had created. The full impact of the artist's delicate shaping of the irises could now be fully appreciated. A short step back, some added distance, had sharpened my view. Everything became clear.

I wrote a poem about a pair of old sneakers and couldn't find a suitable ending. Frustration began to swirl around me. Nothing seemed to be working. I was forcing the words out, and when they finally arrived, they were not landing in the right place. Eventually I put the poem away in a folder and went on with some unrelated reading. I took the dog for a walk along the beach.

As it happened, I didn't return to that poem for quite some time. It was almost a year to the day when I stumbled across it waiting patiently among a pile of unpolished writing pieces – fragments of ideas stored in a notebook for another day. That was distancing myself in the extreme. But in this instance, it worked a treat.

When I reread those initial raw words, I knew exactly how to finish the poem. It was as if the problem had resolved itself in my absence. The distance I had placed between myself and the poem had been productive. My head was clear, my vision restored, and the words presented themselves willingly. Putting distance between yourself and your initial words can prove quite fruitful.

Sneaker Look

Discarded sneakers
Scuffed and mangled
Laces frayed
Twisted
Tangled
Both lay rejected by the door
They'll not see action any more
No more housing smelly socks
Running
Leaping
Scrambling rocks

The sole is smooth
Colour faded
Worn out torn out
Dejected
Jaded
And worst of all
On each sad shoe
Is a giant hole
Where a toe pokes through
Their value has at last diminished
Sad to say
Their sneaking's finished.

Alan j Wright

CONSIDER

For writers, the notion of distance is critical. There are times when we need to step back from our writing to view it more clearly. This deliberate distancing enables us as writers to more fully understand the words initially spread across the page. We afford ourselves a wonderful opportunity to view our words with clarity.

Ask yourself: Do the words on the page match the vision I had in my head? Is this the message I intended? By distancing yourself for an hour, a day even, you are better able to appreciate what needs to happen next. Creating distance enables the writer to return with fresh perspective. It increases the likelihood of your words settling on the page as you intended. After writing, let the words percolate a little before reviewing them. Step away from the words. Allow them to cool off. Then return to them so that you see them through a fresh lens.

7

ARTEFACTS, EPHEMERA AND WRITING IDEAS

I frequently share with young writers how I create a potential topic list by gathering artefacts, treasures, mementoes and curios before photographing them. It's a topic list using images, rather than words, but it works in exactly the same way, providing a stimulus for deeper thinking around writing.

I shared this idea with teachers and students at Rowville Primary School, and one teacher took the idea and really extended it with her class.

Kate challenged students to go home and gather personal artefacts from around their respective homes. They were further encouraged to photograph or draw the selected items. Kate gathered all the student examples and mounted a display that covered the classroom wall. A wall of wonder was instantly created. Curiosity and questions filled the classroom with fresh energy.

The conversation around the wall display aroused much inquiry from students.

- Who owns that?

- What is that?
- Tell me about this…
- I've got one of those!

Gathering such items together in a class display meant that students had so much to share, to borrow from, and to compare. What a rich gathering of potential writing ideas it generated. I loved how Kate had developed this idea.

On one occasion I entered a classroom carrying a paper shopping bag – a simple unadorned brown bag made from recycled paper. 'What's in the bag?' students asked somewhat predictably. Such is the natural curiosity of children. 'All will be revealed in time,' I replied with a wave of my hand and adopting my best magician persona. The children settled on the floor in front of me and our writers' workshop began…

'Do objects have memories?' I asked as I began to retrieve artefacts from the bag to share with these Grade 5 students. I carefully told the back story connected to each item. They listened intently, keen to know more. In turn, I revealed a camera my father used all those years ago, a glass marble left on my desk by a small child, a marble set of dominoes from Mexico, a shell, a magnifying glass and finally a pen. Ah, but no ordinary pen! Oh no. This pen is my pen of choice. It is a Uniball Gel Impact pen with black ink – a pen I choose when writing in my notebook. It feels comfortable in my hand. When I am writing with this pen, words seem to flow more easily. They effortlessly spill across the page.

I don't feel comfortable with fine-point pens. They have a resistance that my heavy hand finds disconcerting. I choose the 1 mm pen that glides and slides across the pages of my writer's notebook. The page disappears under words emerging from my pen. I have a pen friend! I buy them in lots of four. I am fearful of running out of ink. They do not last long, and they cost more than conventional ballpoint pens, but such is my pen obsession. It is not uncommon for me to have three or four lodged in my shirt pocket at any one time. 'Got enough pens?' fellow writers ask. 'I hope so,' I reply.

I was not surprised to discover that a number of these young writers also had definite views on pens. I felt more at ease knowing this.

I share these revelations with the students and encourage them to gather their own artefacts and consider the stories that lie hidden within and around them. I say: 'Draw them. Photograph them. Place photographs of them in your writer's notebook as a tangible reminder of the particular things important to you.' Ideas frequently emerge from the things right in front of us. Ideas exist in things. Things that are often quite close by.

Ephemera – Clip, Collect, Paste

The 'raw stuff' I paste into my notebooks includes an array of what is often referred to as ephemera. That is, printed or written matter not necessarily intended to be retained or preserved. By preserving them in my notebook I am changing the intended destiny of these items. How's that for power?

When I secure these items in my notebook, it's because I want them to last. Their preservation is important to me. I want them to act as memory markers. We writers are magpies, collectors of ephemera. The stuff we rescue may turn out to be important records of life and social customs, popular culture and national events and issues. Who knows? It may also be viewed as treasure by the gatherer, yet insignificant to others. Personal treasure rather than national treasure. These various items assist me to stay in touch with actual experiences. They become markers of my life's journeys.

As I paste new items into my notebook, they speak to me, stimulating my recall. I linger as they announce their potential as future writing ideas.

I often leave space around these items. This allows me to return at a future date to further explore the memories that may later surface. They possess a special magic – a power to reclaim long-forgotten memories.

Sometimes this ephemera just sits between the pages waiting patiently to be rediscovered. I can never be quite sure what piece of 'stuff' I will settle upon in the future. It is only in the critical act of rereading these precious pages that musty memories are given the opportunity to spring to life. Maybe the spark created will explode into words to be shared with a wider audience.

I once found myself delving into a tin of old coins my father had inherited from his father, my grandfather. Many of the coins were over 100 years old. I was fascinated by my find. However, I was even more intrigued by the discovery of an old train ticket nestled under the coins. It was for a journey from Melbourne to Cootamundra in New South Wales. The year was 1952. As I held the ticket, a host of questions immediately arose. Questions I could not hope to answer. Who purchased the ticket? What was the purpose of the journey to Cootamundra? Why was the ticket kept? I had a Cootamundra conundrum of significant proportions. A mystery story was emerging from this tiny, insignificant ticket kept all that time. It had been locked away all those years awaiting discovery. One day I hope to weave this little mystery into a writing piece. Ephemera holds much magic for the writer.

The word 'gleaning' originally referred to the actions of peasants who formed the habit of collecting what was left in the fields following the harvesting of crops. Today, gleaning more accurately refers to the gathering of items discarded or overlooked by others. In a writing context, the writer gleans ideas as they negotiate their world. They collect things they believe have potential to inform their writing lives. They harvest things others frequently overlook.

CONSIDER

The conscious collecting of ephemera is most helpful to the writer. Such items as tickets, business cards, brochures, news clippings and the like act as memory markers. They are anchoring points for the writing mind. They can assist the writer to launch into a fresh writing idea. Other people may view such items as disposable junk. The writer appreciates their potential as treasure to impact a piece of writing. Consider making it a habit to collect, clip and paste such items into your notebook.

8

WRITING ON A BLANK PAGE

Nothing in the world is like this – a bright white page with pale blue lines. The smell of a newly sharpened pencil, the soft hush of it moving finally one day into letters. (Jacqueline Woodson, Brown Girl Dreaming)

I feed my writing in the same way a devoted gardener feeds and nurtures a plot of vegetables or a stand of roses. I find myself immersed in my writer's notebook as much as the days allow. My writing is nourished by my reading. The input is books of my choosing. Books that have waited patiently for me to pull them down from the shelves of my study and joyfully open them. I dive into these books with a zeal borne of impatience. There is never enough time to indulge my reading pleasure, but I try. Books, newspapers, e-reading, fuel my thinking and gently chip away at my ignorance – nourishment for the mind, the heart, the soul. I roll around in this sea of words, savouring them. I delight in the craft of fellow writers and their sublime word usage.

I celebrate individual words and phrases, wishing I had written them myself. I ponder over viewpoints and observations. I eagerly collect memorable words and phrases from my reading experiences and place them in my notebook. These words serve as reminders. They inspire me, urging me on to greater effort. It is valued time in the collection zone. I am conscious of how fortunate I am to have these days.

I always choose my writer's notebooks with deliberate intent. One summer I chose a notebook inspired by renowned author and illustrator Shaun Tan. It had been primarily designed as a sketchbook, having no lines. However, I chose this notebook for that very reason. I wanted to show young writers, particularly those of primary school age, that it is possible to write in a notebook that has no lines. I wanted to prove that the words wouldn't fall off the page, that it was possible to create text in a blank space. If I chose to sketch, then I had that option as well. My sketching, however, is very rudimentary, though occasionally I dabble in doodling. It serves to remind me how important it is to go beyond the comfort zone.

Part of my motivation for using a notebook with unlined pages arose from visiting classrooms where students were using writers' notebooks that were A4 sketchbooks. Each time they were called upon to write, they commenced to rule lines across each page before a single word emerged. This had the effect of slowing down the composition of the text, and the drawn lines tended to impose an artificial word limit on the writing. For me, it was a sad reflection on the process of choice, revealing a lack of self-confidence on the part of the young writers concerned. We model in so many ways.

I urge young writers to view the blank pages of their notebooks as something inviting rather than something daunting and scary. To think of those blank pages as spaces hungry and eager to receive your freshly delivered words is a message worth delivering on a regular basis. I love to watch the blank page disappear under my freshly minted words. It is quite satisfying to observe this transformation of the page. The blank page needs my help. I am ready and willing to assist.

Beating the Blank Page
A Battle-Cry for the Brave Young Writer

Hello blank page
I'm here to let you know
You hold no fear for me
I come prepared
For above all things, I am a mighty writer
A writer armed with fearless words
And clever, tenacious ideas
Your unmarked surface
Your dazzling, papery blankness
Are no match for a word warrior
Such as me
I shall stare you down
I shall annoy you
I shall employ you
I shall destroy you, one word at a time
Watch as the irresistible spread of my words take over
My powerful phrases
My vivid verbs
My agile adjectives
Letter by letter
Bit by bit
Your landscape will be transformed
Your emptiness filled
You hold no fear for me, Blanky-Blank Page
For I remain forever and always – a mighty writer
And I shall stare you down
Take my word for it.

Alan j Wright

The Very Next Notebook

On a shelf in my study sits a growing collection of notebooks of varying sizes. They are pristine. Not a single word has been written in them. They are ready to go. They await my decision. Which notebook will I use next? I like the fact that I have a choice.

Each time I choose a notebook, I consciously choose one that is different from the previous one. Its length, width and thickness all come under scrutiny when making my choice. It's a personal thing. I want each notebook to stand out. I cherish the individuality. I like it to be a little different in shape and form to its predecessor. Even the thickness of the paper comes under scrutiny. Change is good. Choice for the writer begins here. Writers make decisions. Ownership is exercised in the choice of the notebook. I am predictable in many ways, or so I am told, but in this part of my life, change is a compelling force.

Some writers are happy to stick with one style of notebook, so long as it fits their needs as a writer. Me, I like to change the form each time. It spices the writing experience up a little. Each notebook will contain its unique set of words and ideas, so for me, identity is important.

An earlier notebook had an unmistakable cover. It was made from recycled rice bags and recycled paper – quite colourful in appearance and possessed of a pleasant tactile quality. I found myself immediately drawn to it. The pages were made from recycled paper. It had Velcro tabs on pouches for storing important slips of paper and assorted ephemera. It required no additional adornment to show everyone it was mine. I have not seen another notebook like it in my travels. Mind you, it cost me $24 for the privilege of owning this unique volume, but I figured it was worth it. I thoroughly enjoyed our time together as writer and notebook.

Will the next one be the leather-bound volume with unlined recycled-paper pages? Will it be the sturdy A4-sized hard-covered notebook I bought from an office supplies franchise for a mere $5? Will it be smaller, like my current notebook? I currently have quite a stack of differently configured notebooks from which to choose. Some I purchased, others were given to me as gifts. All of them are strong enough to travel and strong enough to withstand the rigours of the writing life. This is where choice begins. I'll let the mood take me. What a pleasant dilemma I face…

I always hold mixed feelings about commencing a new notebook. I am quite excited about the prospect of filling the fresh pages of a brand-new book. I embrace the challenge. To see my words spread out and over the sparkling white pages is a buzz for a writer. It is exciting. I'm involved in the act of capturing the raw stuff of my writing life and bringing order to my messy mind.

With refreshing honesty, a student writer described her feelings when capturing words in her writer's notebook: 'The words rush out of me and are inking onto the page as fast as lightning. When I write, the words rush out like I'm spewing!' (Sarah, Grade 5, Tarneit College).

This harvesting of words and ideas adds to the energy of writing in this new place. But in the end, there is also a sense of loss…

I am farewelling a friend. I am saying goodbye to a travelling companion. The notebook I have just completed has been with me every day for the past few months. Everywhere I have been, it has been there too. It now bulges like a well-fed belly – a notebook chock-a-block with gathered thoughts, ideas and potential treasures to spark more detailed writing pieces.

It will gradually cease to be my travelling companion. As my new notebook begins to fill, it will reach a point where it will contain sufficient content to travel solo. The retired notebook will continue to play an active role in my writing life, though. It will join an ever-expanding library of notebooks I periodically revisit and reread. I am conscious of the vital role rereading plays in informing my writing ideas. It is from reading old entries that new ideas frequently emerge. I will adopt the role of treasure hunter while I reread. I will be spending time with an old friend.

Observing the Not So Obvious

> The question is not what you look at, but what you see.
> *(Henry David Thoreau, 1962)*

Learning to be a keen observer is not only critical to writing development but has implications for developing one's world knowledge. This knowledge needs to incorporate meaning and understanding, rather than mere surface knowledge.

If we want student writers to notice things they encounter in their world, we must actively teach into this. After all, they are part of an acutely visual generation. They are bombarded with images – so many, in fact, that the task of determining importance becomes even more difficult. The continuing challenge for teachers remains this: How do we assist young writers to grow as discriminating viewers of their various worlds? How do we as adults do this – sort the wheat from the chaff?

Developing a writer's keen eye for observation will serve the young writer well in a media-saturated world. The more we notice, the more we are likely to grow and learn.

It is important for every writer to develop a keen sense of observation. When a teacher is a keen observer of the world, students find themselves in the company of an awareness mentor.

Our keenest observation takes place when we are not preoccupied with other matters. Sometimes it requires self-talk to refocus our energy on our immediate surroundings and declutter our overcrowded minds. We must learn to observe consciously – something that takes practice.

Ralph Fletcher encourages writers to push beyond the sight of things and look at other less glamorous senses such as smell, taste and touch when making observations. This is an invitation with significant appeal. The curious learner is thus challenged to broaden the possibilities with regard to their respective responses. It makes sense…

Close observation is vital. The writer may listen for snatches of conversation. On a train, at the park, in a shop, sitting drinking coffee – snatches of conversation float in the air, awaiting discovery and capture. The writer notices simple behaviours – quirky, bizarre, fleeting, mundane – and captures them. This harvesting of behaviour brings with it a buzz. The writer remains ever ready to catch these sometimes-fleeting moments. Among those gatherings may lie treasure…

The seemingly unspectacular is duly noted by the writer who draws attention to it, making the experience worthy of another look, further consideration. I noted this small observation in my notebook while sitting in a coffee shop: 'He tugged gently at his beard as if to ensure it was secure.'

Look at small things. Remember, a piece of writing is about *something*. That doesn't mean the subject needs to be grandiose. 'My sister turned and left the room without saying a word.' That's a story. Particularly if the sister in question is not known for silent departures.

Sometimes you find yourself in the right place at the right time…

> I grew up in the Dandenong Ranges surrounded by hills, valleys, creeks, forests and ferns of extraordinary size. It was a huge backyard. Exploring this damp, green space remained an endless pleasure. On one expedition round about the age of 12, I wandered into the forest below our house and walked the track meandering beside the Sassafras Creek. I was intent on checking out potential fishing spots. The forest around me was briefly quiet, allowing the flow of the creek to be clearly heard. It was the prime moving force in the forest. It flowed on, murmuring a soft flub-flub as it cornered the bank. The water surface rippled gently, clear and cold. Suddenly a mid-sized fish, a rainbow trout, I suspect, exploded through the surface of the stream, heaving its speckled glimmering body upwards, as if shot from a cannon. It disappeared with a watery slap of bubbles and foam. A flash, a flicker, a gravity defying leap, then the performance was over. The surface of the water quickly repaired. The calm instantly reinstated. Natural order restored, the creek and the fish flowed on. I saw it though. I was there in that moment in

the forest when a fish frolicked. I found myself in a privileged position. A front row seat had enabled me to witness a simple pleasure. A fleeting moment in time, I will remember forever. This is what made growing up in this place so special. The art of observation has its origins in retaining such moments. Being ready to receive and retain these ephemeral flashes and flecks of time help to set a writer apart.

Learn to breathe in the world wherever you happen to be. Writing is at its best when the writer aims to get up close to the topic or subject. It requires the writer to note small, yet critical details. The noting of small, seemingly insignificant detail brings the writing into sharper focus. It offers the reader a window seat. Writers become more adept at close noticing only through mindful practice. The aim is to become a practised observer of the world.

Writers must also practice the art of specificity. When generalities are used, the reader gets a partially developed view. Learning to take your writing from the general to the specific sharpens the reader's view and deepens their understanding. I consciously practice re-reading my words in order to notice where the writing is vague or lacking focus. I search for meaning and details below the surface of these general words.

I learned so much from reading Annie Dillard's Pulitzer Prize-winning book *Pilgrim at Tinker Creek* recounting her close observations over the course of a year in the Blue Ridge Valley of Virginia. It is an astonishing record of the mysterious and the beautiful encounters she experienced. I have read and reread this amazing book. I read it slowly and deliberately. I continue to dive into it across random pages. I want the words to soak into me. Dillard's language is both peppery and poetic. I want to learn from her incredible ability to observe what others fail to see.

> I leaned to examine the white thing and saw a mass of bubbles like spittle. Then I saw something dark like an engorged leech rummaging over the spittle, and then I saw the praying mantis.

She was upside down, clinging to a horizontal stem of wild rose by her feet which pointed to heaven. Her head was deep in dried grass. Her abdomen was swollen like a smashed finger; it tapered off to a fleshy point out of which bubbled a wet, whipped froth. (Dillard, 1974)

In *A Writer's Notebook: Unlocking the Writer Within*, Ralph Fletcher (1996b) notes: 'If you get in the habit of paying attention to your world and writing down what you notice, your notebook will fill up with lots of intriguing stuff...'

CONSIDER

In *Once Upon A Slime: 45 Fun Ways to Get Writing... FAST*, author Andy Griffiths (2013) gives this sound advice to writers:

> Sometimes the easiest way to start writing is not to try to 'think something up' but to simply 'Write something down' – and what better place to begin than with what is right in front of your eyes!

It is advice worthy of our attention as writers.

9

THE SPARK OF AN IDEA

Creativity is a continual surprise. (Ray Bradbury, Zen in the Art of Writing, 2015)

Inexperienced writers are often unsure where to find potential writing ideas. They frequently ask, 'Where do you find writing ideas?'

I am tempted to be flippant and tell them I visit a little writing ideas shop located in the Melbourne suburb of Moonee Ponds, where a delightful old couple dole them out, one at a time, from a locker hidden deep in their basement – but I don't…

The real answer lies hidden right before their eyes – ideas exist all around us. They are hiding in the open. We must let student writers in on this little secret. The inexperienced writer frequently overlooks possibilities simply because they are not practised observers. Sharing how a more experienced writer determines what they will write about and how they will present their writing ideas is an essential part of developing self-directed, confident and independent writers.

So, where might we begin?

A writer's life experiences are an important starting point. Every writer should be encouraged to tell the unique stories of their life. These special experiences have so much potential for launching writing in the classroom. Apart from talking about their lives, young writers should be encouraged to share what they discovered from the experience. These vignettes hold much potential for propelling writing forward. They say much about success and failure, life lessons, and the full gamut of human emotions. The secret lies in getting young writers talking and sharing. In time the inexperienced writer will begin to value these experiences as rich fodder for writing.

A writer may play many roles, but mostly they are storytellers. They often tell their stories many times before they actually begin to write them. For many writers, this forms part of rehearsal for writing. This makes the telling of stories within the classroom and beyond an essential piece of the puzzle. Each of us has many, many stories inside our head just awaiting discovery. This storytelling requires a space in which to thrive. It is therefore incumbent on teachers to set up for the sharing of these stories. It creates an environment that feeds ideas and launches possibilities.

It is equally important to assist the inexperienced writer in identifying the broad influences and interests surrounding their lives. Nancie Atwell (1987) referred to these as 'writing territories' in her book *In the Middle: Writing, Reading, and Learning with Adolescents*.

Writing Territories

Writing territories are the broad range of things we know most about, as well as the influences on our lives. Hobbies and interests are part of our territories. Consider also genres, audiences and subjects that most appeal to each of us when we choose to write. Within these broad territories, specific topics lie waiting to be uncovered. We must encourage the young writer to explore their specific territories in order to seek out topics and ideas worthy of attention:

- They should only write about those things they care about.
- They should be writing with a reader/readers in mind.
- They should write to discover, uncover, explore, share and understand themselves and their world.

It is important to firmly establish in the minds of student authors that writers do a lot more than just write stories. Developing a broader concept of what it means to be a writer will hopefully benefit your students as they strive to gain confidence. Here are some of the roles writers may adopt:

The Roles a Writer May Play

- Writers are recorders/reporters.
- Writers learn from other writers.
- Writers wonder.
- Writers write about the unexpected and unusual.
- Writers remember the past.
- Writers are storytellers.
- Writers investigate and collect facts.
- Writers send messages.
- Writers read in order to write.
- Writers write regularly.
- Writers experiment.
- Writers reread and rewrite.
- Writers are poets.
- Writers explain.
- Writers write about special moments.
- Writers collect words as well as writing they admire.
- Writers are curious observers.
- Writers frequently rehearse before they write.
- Writers persuade.

- Writers describe.
- Writers explain things.
- Writers inspire others.
- Writers notice little things others often miss.
- Writers don't always begin at the start.
- Writers daydream and imagine.
- Writers write about people and places.
- Writers write both short and long pieces.
- Writers work to influence our thinking.
- Writers reveal their point of view or bias.

The Way Forward with Brainstorming

Brainstorming is a strategy that has many learning applications. I want to specifically look at brainstorming within the context of writing workshops and how we can assist developing writers to use it more effectively.

It would be inaccurate to think of pre-writing as merely brainstorming, though from my observations many teachers do, unfortunately. This is not to say that brainstorming is not a critical pre-writing skill for young writers to acquire. In fact, it provides an excellent way to deepen student thinking around a new topic. It activates prior knowledge critical to writing success. Brainstorming allows the writer to generate ideas before organising them. The challenge remains how to do it most effectively.

Brainstorming is often viewed as problematic. Concerns are frequently voiced over what is perceived as student inability to generate ideas when asked to brainstorm as a pre-writing activity.

What often occurs is that students are asked to think of as many ideas as they can around a topic or idea, and the result is a minimal list more recognisable as *drizzle* than brainstorm. 'How come they can't do this?' teachers frequently ask.

Well, let's look at what happens when young writers are initially asked to brainstorm. Watching the inexperienced writer 'brainstorm' is revealing. They frequently indulge in what might be termed 'self-censoring' or 'editing out' of potential ideas. In other words, they think of ideas/connections and then immediately discount them for fear of writing down the wrong answer. In brainstorming, there are no wrong answers. They hesitate for fear of making mistakes. They apply judgments to their ideas before they are even hatched. This apparent lack of confidence or faith in their ideas may also result from choosing a topic they know little about. The resulting list contains predictable responses. Young writers are frequently invited to brainstorm before they have been shown how this important strategy actually works.

The most experienced, proficient writer in the room needs to step forward at this point of the lesson and reveal the secrets of successful brainstorming. In the same way that a magician reveals special magic to an audience, the writing teacher needs to create some sparks around brainstorming.

Let's begin…

Adopt the notion of 'show, don't tell' when revealing the brainstorming strategy to young writers. Begin by saying something like, 'Young writers, watch me closely as I explore my thinking around a topic of interest.'

Ask the students gathered before you to time you as you document your thinking in front of them. It is important for them to experience your thinking in action. Use a think-aloud strategy, so the thoughts in your head are shared. After the allotted time (say three minutes), ask your writing audience to provide feedback on what they saw you doing and heard you saying.

You will probably receive comments similar to this:

- 'You worked really quickly.'
- 'You were concentrating on your ideas.'
- 'You made a list' (my preferred style for documenting my thinking).

- 'You reread your ideas to get new ones.'
- 'You wrote down almost everything that came into your head.'
- 'You didn't cross anything out.'
- 'You made a long list.'
- 'You didn't stop thinking and writing.'
- 'You asked yourself questions.'

Document the feedback you receive on a chart to draw attention to the brainstorming behaviours students have noted. This is such an important part of the process. Inform them that the next step would be to organise and refine the listed items. Ask, 'Do I have to use every listed item?' They will begin to understand that you are not obligated to do this. They will also understand that, because you have many listed ideas, there are more options at your disposal.

When I demonstrate in this way, I always sense an immediate change in the group. They are ready and primed to try this for themselves. The change is palpable. It is prudent to advise students to choose a topic they feel they know a lot about. That way, students are more likely to dive straight in when their turn arrives. The challenge of the blank page is destroyed under a flurry of words and phrases, clustering, mind maps, etc. I love it! When teachers see this change take place, they are often astounded that such growth in thinking appears to have taken place in the blink of an eye.

The brainstorming demonstration is without doubt transformational. It is yet another example of the power of allowing the inexperienced writer to witness, up close and personal, how a particular aspect of the pre-writing process is conducted by an experienced writer. I am never disappointed by the response!

Never lose sight of the fact that the aim of brainstorming is quantity before quality. We want developing writers to deeply explore their thinking without any judgmental overlay. They should delay judgment until the list is produced. If they do this, something of interest is more likely to bubble to the surface. The lists will be far more extensive, and the likelihood of divergent thinking will be enhanced.

Brainstorming used in conjunction with other pre-writing strategies greatly enhances the likelihood that the writing students produce will be of a higher quality when it eventually appears on the page. Now, that's a worthy outcome to pursue!

CONSIDER

Read

Reading is an excellent way to discover potential writing ideas.

- What do other writers write about?
- How do they write about specific topics and themes?
- What genres do they mostly choose when writing about certain topics?

When young writers are encouraged to explore such questions, they are significantly closer to finding what it is they truly wish to say as writers.

Observe

Encourage student writers to more effectively engage with their surroundings. Give them cameras or provide them with materials and time for sketching. Discuss the finer detail of these images. Ask them to describe what is just beyond the image. Lock in these observations by encouraging discussion and see where it leads the writer. Link this work to the work of photographers and illustrators. Explore the world from a variety of angles.

Collect

Collect artefacts and ephemera in notebooks as a stimulus for writing. Writers are collectors.

10

INVESTIGATE TO STIMULATE

> You are an explorer. Your mission is to document and observe the world around you as if you've never seen it before. Take notes, collect things you find on your travels. Document your findings. Notice patterns. Copy. Trace. Focus on one thing at a time. Record what you are drawn to. *(Keri Smith, How To Be an Explorer of the World, 2008)*

When we embark upon an investigation of how writers write, why they write and how they use notebooks to stimulate the writing lives they lead, we become better informed as writers ourselves.

If we investigate how other writers choose topics, identify writing projects, and undertake the various processes of writing in order to make their writing 'reader friendly', we gain insight and understanding. We may ask: 'What did the author need to do in order to be able to write a particular text? What prior knowledge did the author need?' At any time, 'Why?' is a powerful question to ask.

Each of these actions will be even more effective if the most proficient writer in the classroom – the writing teacher – mindfully demonstrates a curiosity around these investigative behaviours, so as to tease out critical knowledge about writing. It adds a necessary gravitas to writing.

As a writer, I have never woken up thinking, 'Today I'll write a persuasive essay!' I know instinctively what kind of writing I am creating by engaging in the very act of composing words. If I'm writing an article for a magazine, the words 'expository writing' never enter my mind at the time of writing. Writers don't think of their writing in such terms. No writer chooses a text type merely to practise it.

It seems we only talk about writing this way in the 'school world'. Curriculum documents and assessment guides abound with words like 'persuasive', 'procedural' and 'narrative'. Would you go to your local library and ask the librarian to guide you to the 'procedural texts'?

These terms are used to define writing instruction, and are rarely challenged. Don't we want writing to be as individual as the creators of those words? Don't we want the product to be as unique as the person producing it?

For this reason, young writers should be encouraged to write about topics close to their hearts and to write in a manner of their own choosing. They decide if they have something important and interesting to say about the subject or idea. In this scenario the teacher guides and supports the developing writer to make informed choices regarding the form and shape the writing might take.

Too often students write about issues and ideas they either know little about or care little about. They need guidance and support to find ideas that reside closer to the heart. Katie Wood-Ray (2006), in her book *Study Driven*, poses the question that needs to be asked at this point: 'What have I read in the world that is like what I am trying to write?'

Many books are hybrid in nature. They employ a number of modes. When writing *Igniting Writing: When a Teacher Writes* (Wright, 2011), I employed several modes. Part of it is in a narrative mode, where I use stories to illustrate certain situations and to explain my writing life. I certainly devote a large portion of the book to conveying information considered important to the reader. Further to this, I also engage in writing that is procedural, aims to persuade or is descriptive. I write in these different modes to help me achieve my ultimate writing goals.

In many schools the teaching of writing has been oversimplified. Writing is viewed like one would view a recipe. In attempting to control the messy beast we call writing, it is frequently segregated and compartmentalised. Genres becomes isolated into unrelated entities in order to simplify and control the writing. The writing landscape becomes dotted with silos, each one representing a discrete and separate genre.

Encouraging students to include whatever mode is important for them to convey their writing ideas would seem a more natural approach. Narrative can be used extensively in writing and is a very effective tool for building a reader's interest in all kinds of writing. Cynthia Rylant (1995) combines poetry and narrative in The Van Gogh Café. Morris Gleitzman (2001) includes an email format in his narrative story *Adults Only*.

There was a time when cookbooks were exclusively procedural. Now I buy hybrid cookery texts. My appetite as a reader and a food lover is satisfied by such varied approaches. The procedural aspects of the recipe writing are frequently accompanied by photographs and anecdotes related to the evolution of that specific recipe, or family stories that mark historical connections to the recipe. These add zest to the writing and broaden the appeal for the reader. Some of my favourite food writers, such as Yotam Ottolenghi, Guy Mirabella and Jamie Oliver, write in this style. They share the story surrounding the food, thus providing the reader with a stronger connection. I have frequently used such texts to demonstrate that writing is innately more interesting when the writer embraces a range of genres. The author chooses to be genre-promiscuous.

When showing students pieces of writing believed to qualify as exemplary, it is critical to ask:

- 'What is the writer doing here to convey a message?'

- 'Have you read other pieces that look and sound like this?'
- 'Have you read a different kind of text on the same subject or theme?'
- 'What are you noticing that the writer is doing that you wish you could do?'
- 'Why would an author do something like that?'

I discovered these pertinent comments from an anonymous blogger on the subject of choice and genre:

> I want children who do not shy away from writing, children who hear it is time for writing workshop and get excited, a time of day where they can be themselves, share a message, tell their story – in whatever way they wish. I think about how we teach reading. Children read books that are appropriate for them; books that are 'just right' and that they are interested in. We don't dictate genres in reading, should we in writing? I hear a lot about what we want the students to write, what we think they should write, what genres they 'need' to write. I don't hear us asking, let alone listening to the kids – finding out what type of writing they want to do. We claim there is choice… but are we really providing choice? *('writingteach', https://writingteach.edublogs.org)*

Let's Not Forget

Providing students with choice, promoting ownership, and helping students draw on their own experience, interests and inquiry engages them as writers. It must be recognised that not all students have to write with the same purpose, or for the same audience at the same time.

When students write about issues, needs, problems or subjects they consider important and relevant to them as writers, we improve the odds for their engagement, as well as the likelihood that they will strive to write well. Under the teacher's guidance, students can be encouraged to conduct inquiries into matters of interest to them, generating ideas and questions and analysing problems and issues. From such inquiries, students develop writing that communicates their ideas for different purposes and audiences. Hopefully, it reveals itself in different forms.

The more a young writer owns a topic, the more likely they are to write. The more they write, the more they discover. Making choices is a skill. We need to give developing writers opportunities to engage in this kind of considered thinking if we, as educators, are serious about fostering independent thoughts and ideas.

Exploring My Immediate World

When possible, I like to walk in the morning air not too long after the sun has peeped above the far horizon. Before the birds have ceased their morning song. Before the dogs have found a spot in the sun, and before the morning dew has completely gone. When I find myself on holiday, I feel compelled to walk more frequently.

On one such morning, though, as part of my summer writes, I followed the lead of Keri Smith (2008) in her book *How To Be an Explorer of the World* and set out on my morning walk with the words 'Everything is interesting – look closer' singing in my ears. My project was to take photos only of things found on the ground. Using my smartphone, I walked the familiar streets of my neighbourhood, pausing to snap items that caught my eye.

Since the age of about ten I have been enamoured by photography. As a teacher and a writer, this love of the photographic image has been a positive influence. It has aided my eye as a writer. Small detail is important. What takes place inside a camera can also take place inside your head.

As a teacher of writing, I need to view myself as a collector. I must observe, collect and analyse. This documentation of specific elements of my immediate world and culture is my life-source. I also collect to enable me to remember. Sometimes I collect things that initially appear meaningless or trivial. However, the reflective process of writing often leads me back to an important realisation or wider connection. In the process, I am better informed as a writer.

In order for student writers to grow into close observers of their world, they must be led into new territories and methods of investigation. So, as I set out on my mission, I found myself acutely focused.

The images I capture on my walk become potential writing topics and ideas. When I take such deliberate action, it assists me in achieving the vital link to new ideas.

This little observation project had me thinking about my next visual project. Maybe the next focus (pardon the pun) could be 'things on walls'. This was fun. It was easy and it was instructive. My summer writes will continue. These images will be placed into my notebook. They will serve to inform me as a writer. Anything can be a starting place…

Noticings – A Writer's Life Source

Part of the writer's role is to draw attention to the details of the world. For this reason, writers need to develop a capacity for keen observation.

Think for a moment what this means for teaching student writers. Teaching writing needs to delve way beyond structural considerations. If teaching energy remains focused solely on the mechanics of writing, the writing will remain functional at best. It will undoubtedly lack voice and precision.

A teacher who assists the developing writer to grow as an observer, to connect strongly to the world in which they operate, provides the student writer with vital skills they can apply, not just to the writing they undertake, but to learning in general. Developing the writer as observer creates an all-round curious learner. To teach writing in this way empowers the writer, empowers the learner.

In order to become the model of a vigilant writer, the writing teacher must practise detailed observation. Such observations become critical sharing events in the classroom. The young writer needs to be exposed to a world of possibility. This world of possibility must be revealed to student writers. They deserve no less.

The writer who closely observes strives to make the everyday aspects of the world sparkle with renewed appeal for the reader. They write in ways that aim to shake the reader out of complacency, alerting them to such possibility. As Ralph Fletcher (1996b) states, 'Writers react.' They react to the various things they encounter as they go about their lives. They notice and record things other people pass by, dismiss or discard.

Writers also notice the range of human emotions that pervade life. They record the various aspects of mood swirling around them as they negotiate each day: anger, happiness, irritation, contemplation. When a writer becomes acutely aware of the emotional world, they are better placed to describe such feelings with greater authenticity and understanding. Learning to write with such descriptive honesty enables readers to see themselves in the words conveyed.

Jerry Spinelli (1990) uses the craft strategy – show don't tell – to accurately capture the extent of Amanda's anger in this passage from his award-winning book *Maniac Magee*:

> Amanda cried. She tore a magazine in half. She punched the sofa. She kicked the easy chair. She kicked Bow Wow. Bow Wow went yelping into the kitchen. 'See!' she yelled at the front door. 'See what you made me do, Jeffrey Magee! Jeffrey Maniac Crazy Man Bozo Magee!'

As teachers of writing, we must alert student writers to the ways writers capture small moments and add small details to illuminate and write with precision.

While reading the young-adult verse novel *Another Night in Mullet Town*, by Steven Herrick (2016), I was taken by the author's keen observational skills and attention to fine detail. I suggest reading this extract aloud:

IN THE SOFT LIGHT

After spinach pie
and mashed potato,
with the rain echoing
on the corrugated roof,
and Dad somewhere
between here and Adelaide,
Mum sits at the kitchen table
with a small jar of red nail polish.
I watch as she files her nails
to a smooth round tip.
Delicate veins
thread along the back of her hands.
The fumes make my eyes water
as Mum applies a second coat
to the nails of her left hand
even though
she hasn't touched the ones
on her right.
She carefully blows the polish dry,
then hands me the jar
and extends her right hand.
I dip the brush into the polish
and apply a thick smear
to her little finger.
We don't speak
all my effort focused on her nails,
red and glowing,
in the soft light of the evening.

A Curious Learner

I shall remain
A curious learner
All the days of my life
All the wondrous ways of the world
Are mine to explore
I retain an urge for
Poking around, probing, prying and unpacking
Exploring new places
Embracing ideas
Taking risks
Turning things over
Peering around corners
Rummaging with relish
Looking over walls
I will wander and wonder
All the days of my life
Curiosity, the engine driving me
Towards discovery
And new knowledge
Chipping away at my ignorance
A chunk at a time.

Alan j Wright

CONSIDER

The ability to read like writers develops by noticing the craft moves of writers we encounter in our reading lives. Such a reading skill requires practice and only develops with time. A teacher's noticing of such word treasure is essential if student writing is to benefit from the crafted moves of more experienced writers.

In order to do this most effectively, we too must learn to pay attention, be alert to possibility. We must learn to collect scraps of detail in our notebooks as we negotiate the days of our lives. Noticing is a writer's essential connection to their readers.

As teachers of writing, we do our students a disservice if we don't draw attention to these important aspects of writing. Under the banner 'Words I wish I'd written', begin collecting extracts you might use in your teaching: writing moves young writers can imitate and hopefully innovate upon.

11

YIELDING TO THE INFLUENCE OF OTHER WRITERS

> All great literary works influence us as writers, not their stories as much as their storytelling ability. *(Michael Scott, Interview with Erin Underwood, 2011)*

Australian singer, songwriter and storyteller Paul Kelly was once asked where he found ideas, and he answered, 'I steal them.'

Kelly was being somewhat self-effacing, but he was also close to a truth all writers know. They know what imitation looks like. Such influences are unavoidable.

At some stage in our writing journey we try on other voices, adopting then adapting them. Such influences are important to our development as writers. We may find ourselves drawn to the rhythm, description or structure of the words. This influence on our ears and eyes is inevitable. The more we read as writers, the more we are exposed to the influence of our fellow writers.

I read somewhere: 'Bad writers borrow, good writers steal.' When you notice yourself influenced by the words of another writer, you need to shape that influence to make it fit your writing intentions and your particular voice.

In my previous book, *Igniting Writing: When a Teacher Writes*, I wrote at length about how I have been informed by the writing of Jerry Spinelli and his influence on my work, particularly his use of repetition and short, punchy sentences (Wright, 2011). Roald Dahl's wonderful character descriptions are another influential craft consideration I find compelling. At various times, I have been conscious of writing under the influence of both Spinelli and Dahl.

Writing in the style of another author is something we need to practise as teachers of writing. By experiencing the influence of a mentor on our writing, we are better positioned to 'show' our students how this act of writing in the style of another author can influence writing, nudging it forward.

Some teachers express concern that inviting students to write in the style of an author they admire will result in 'copying'. The modelling we do as teachers is a critical element in this aspect of writing. By example, we show how we imitate the style, not the content. This type of powerful demonstration is essential. Again, it employs the notion of 'show, don't tell' to influence change. Our student writers need to see how it is done by a more proficient writer.

In his 2014 book *Brilliant*, Roddy Doyle devotes his writing attention to the mumbling of adults with great effect:

> The house was full of mumbles these days. Mumbles that often stopped whenever Raymond or Gloria walked into the room. Mumbling was what grown ups did when they thought they were whispering. Whispers only stayed in the air for a little while, but mumbles rolled around for ages, high in the corners, along the window frames, all around the house. The mumbles had almost become creatures.

This attention to small detail lifts the writing to a higher plain. My writer's eye is drawn to such meticulous attention to a seemingly small matter.

Doyle alerts the reader to the significance of the act of mumbling and its impact on the characters. He draws a distinction between whispering and mumbling. He highlights the writing craft in this passage. The words jumped off the page when I read them. I immediately reread them. I pondered the words and felt this was something worth noting in my writer's notebook. This is writing to which I aspire.

Writing in the style of another writer can often lead to discoveries – discoveries about characters and events you actually want to write about. It may lead you to the story you need to write. I urge you to try it for your students' sake.

Try these ideas in the safety of your own writer's notebook before sharing them with your students:

> Select a passage/extract from a text you find appealing. How would you write it differently? Maybe you could change the setting, the tone, or redefine the character/s.

> Select a piece from a mentor text that provides you with a strong sense of voice. Rewrite it, heightening or exaggerating the voice.

Assisting Young Writers to Find Treasure

I found myself closely examining the content gathered across the pages of my writer's notebooks over the years. It led me to thinking about what I have seen in a multitude of kids' notebooks across the last 20 years or so. What struck me as significant was the almost total absence of words gathered from potential writing mentors.

These young writers appear to have been left out of the loop when it comes to the treasure awaiting them in the books they read – treasure their eyes and minds wander past almost daily. Nobody rang to alert them to these collectible word treasures. They don't read like writers and that's such a shame...

I am a frequent gatherer of words I wish I had written – words from fellow writers, both inspiring and thought-provoking. I consider it important for student writers to view this type of gathering as a legitimate activity. My writer's notebooks regularly reflect this passion for gathering word treasure. Our notebooks have space to accommodate those words possessing the power to rub off on our own words.

The words I collect from other authors sit among my own words. That way, my words are hanging out with the best possible examples of writing. I want my words to be thinking, 'Wow, I want to be like that!'

When our eyes fall upon words we identify as wondrous, we should copy them into our notebooks as a reminder of powerful and inspirational writing. These words are the words *we wish we had written...*

When sharing my harvest of notebook entries, I frequently say things like:

> 'I love that line – let me tell you why.'
>
> 'Listen to the sounds of that magical sentence. Can you hear it too?'
>
> 'What great description of the setting. I can see that so clearly in my mind.'

An emotional response to the writing of others is important to acknowledge within yourself, as a reader. It is also important to share these responses with less experienced readers and writers. When we are moved or provoked by the words on the page, the writer has done their job. We must show the less experienced writer how we engage with the words of other writers.

As writers and teachers of writing, we need to develop a close relationship with those authors we admire. We need to get close to their words. We need to study aspects of their craft closely. We need to learn to savour their words. We need to learn to read, not just with our eyes, but also with our ears, our hearts. Reading like a writer requires a coordinated effort within each of us. These authors (and illustrators) can become our mentors. We can be lifted by their wings.

The passages and extracts I copy into my notebook regularly come from those writers I view as mentors and heroes. Their words inspire me to greater efforts as a writer. I write under their influence, I write in their style. Sometimes, I include extracts that serve as reminders to write in a certain way.

Such writers can, in time, become our unwitting collaborators in teaching more effectively. Armed with such knowledge, teachers of writing can more confidently assist the inexperienced writer to begin appreciating how the quality of writing immeasurably improves when we instinctively allow quality writing to impact our own work as writers. This is where the essential skill of reading like a writer emerges.

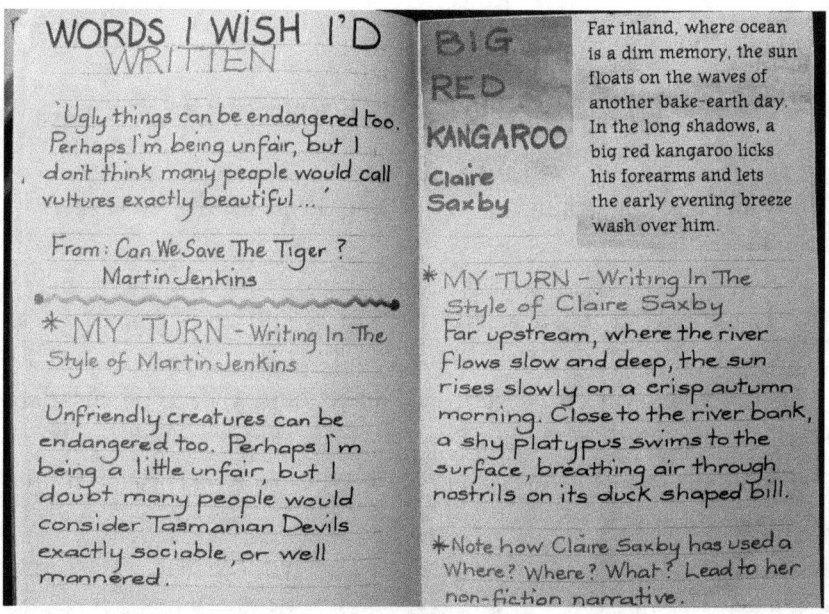

Many young and inexperienced writers have not been in the habit of working in their notebooks in this way. This approach is often new to them. They have not been opened up to such influences.

A Matter of Heavy Sentences

Have you ever noticed how sometimes, when you read, you come to a sentence that makes you keen to know more? Some sentences have a lot of ideas packed inside them. They prompt the asking of questions. You just know that if you were able to open them up like a suitcase there would be more interesting things to discover.

If we can identify those sentences heavy with hidden ideas, we provide ourselves with opportunities to unpack them and share such magic with other readers and writers.

Inexperienced student writers frequently write sentences begging to be unpacked. All too often, their readers are left hanging because the writer fails to unpack the loaded words. The curious reader is left unfulfilled. Experienced writers undertake such craft moves regularly. Here are some heavy sentences written by Morris Gleitzmann. Notice the way Morris follows up and unpacks them in the sentences that follow. He is a master at this aspect of writing craft and offers much in the way of writing treasure to share with young writers.

> **I wake up.** My neck is stiff, and my eyes hurt in the sunlight, and I've got breadcrumbs stuck to my face. *(Morris Gleitzmann, Boy Overboard)*

> **She looks totally exhausted.** Even in this faint light I can see how pale she is, hair plastered round her face, scooping with her eyes closed. Her lips are blue. *(Morris Gleitzmann, Boy Overboard)*

Here are some more examples I uncovered while undertaking some reading as a text detective:

> **McNabb was a giant.** He stood five feet eight and said to weigh over and seventy pounds. He had to bring his birth certificate into the League Director to prove he was only twelve. And still most people didn't believe it.' *(Jerry Spinelli, Maniac Magee)*

Edward started training twice as hard. Instead of eight kilometres, he swam sixteen. Instead of twenty minutes of exercises, he did forty. *(Morris Lurie, The Twenty-Seventh Annual African Hippopotamus Race)*

It was always bedlam at our house. Valjoy was forever slamming out the front door hollering that she was going, this time for good, and not to expect her home ever again. And mum would yell after her that it was the best news she'd heard since she won the fridge in the football club raffle and good riddance – only she didn't mean it. And in the background Jedda would be whinnying or watching the TV racing results with the sound turned up full blast. *(Robin Klein, Hating Alison Ashley)*

As we read, we must look for examples of how other writers unpack their heavy sentences. I frequently copy some examples into my writer's notebook. I also consciously share them with other writers. I suggest reading some of your own writing to see if you can identify where you might need to unpack a heavy sentence or two.

An example of unpacking a heavy sentence:

My uncle took me to the park.

Unpack:

My uncle took me to the park, where we had the best time climbing and playing. He chased me around and around the slides and platforms. After all of that running I needed a break, so we stopped for lunch. What a great time we had!

CONSIDER

Find your own trusted and true unwitting collaborators – those authors you rely upon for inspiration. In the beginning, you might decide to write in the style of these literary giants. In time, you may feel sufficiently confident to innovate and write in a style of your own choosing. We all need scaffolding in the early stages of a learning journey.

To complement this writing action, continue to practise reading like a writer. Such reading will build your capacity for identifying craft moves worthy of attention.

12

THE BOOK OF REVELATIONS

Writer Joan Didion said our (writer's) notebooks give us away. We are revealed by the contents. Our notebooks are a place to collect and then take those collected items and use them to spark further original writing.

With these thoughts ringing in my ears, I envisage notebooks brimming with words and ideas across a range of subjects and genres. The notebook is a place to experiment, take risks, make important discoveries or excavate memories and ideas from deep within. It can be a place to have fun with words and ideas. There is a randomness that pervades all this gathering and collecting.

However, in too many classrooms, when students take out their notebooks, a quick scan through the pages reveals a picture far removed from the one I just outlined. Why does one get the impression that the notebook in these classrooms is only realising a small part of its potential?

Why is the critical ingredient – writing – almost missing in action? Content is so critical to the developing writer, and yet the writers' notebooks in these contexts lack integrity because they're not being used to generate authentic writing.

What does one see documented in these notebooks? Well, usually a couple of pictures, maybe a few artefacts, lists, Y charts, plans, graphic organisers, but very little genuine writing!

A closer examination of the few notebook entries reveals the sad fact that these young writers are writing about the same topic in pretty much the same way. Standardisation is a sad global phenomenon. Think about fast-food standardisation for a moment and the way it has been rolled out across the globe with hideous consequences for consumers. Standardisation conjures a picture of something prepared in an industrial fashion, on a large scale, with standard ingredients and standardised production methods – a sterile sameness. It is concerning when that same sterility infiltrates the teaching of writing. The teacher's need to control writing outranks the need to nurture the growth of writing. The writer's notebook becomes another book in which the inexperienced writer does 'work' sent their way by an adult. That adult exerts power over what goes in the notebook. The teacher's topics reign supreme! The writer's notebook takes on the appearance of a stage-managed planning book, rather than a place to write, experiment and take risks. When student notebooks take on this appearance, it is obvious that writing is not the major focus of such managed creations.

It is important to stress the importance of providing opportunities for students to write independently on a daily basis. Students must be consistently encouraged to think of things to write about. They will rise to the challenge, especially if they know their teachers support such efforts.

A significant number of teachers are non-writers themselves, and this feeds a reluctance to trust. In this scenario, the teacher frequently experiences great difficulty 'giving over' the control of writing to their students. The student writers are frequently instructed what to write, and it amounts to little more than listen and respond. The writing program in such classrooms is reduced to students writing to a 'prompt' – a prompt owned and provided by the teacher.

I still have strong memories of my own Grade 5 teacher imposing a weekly writing topic on our class. I recall with little joy writing about 'My Life as a Pen' and 'Autobiography of an Ant'. The teacher prowled the room as we wrote on 'her' topic of choice. Our 'composition' books were collected at the conclusion of the allotted writing time, taken away and corrected in isolation. When returned the following week, they were covered in red ink where she had vigorously corrected our writing. Bloodshed on the page. There was no other feedback, apart from a mark out of ten. We only found out what was wrong with our writing. There was never any attempt to build on what we knew about writing.

All our teacher's effort on correction was largely a waste of time. Writing grew to be associated with negative outcomes. The only time we wrote was on those dreaded Thursday afternoons.

Those early experiences as a writer continue to motivate me to provide explicit feedback and support for young writers at every stage of the writing process. They need to feel that their efforts to develop as writers will be valued. By doing this, each child is more likely to achieve what they set out to do when they commence writing.

I have been told on numerous occasions: 'This is where my students do their thinking. They do their writing in a writing draft book!' A disconnect exists here.

I have always believed that it is in my writing that I reveal my initial thinking, and if I have a writer's notebook, why do I need an additional book in which to commence my writing? It seems redundant. My notebook is my launching pad for writing ideas. It contains many beginnings. I am able to select from those beginnings a piece which I identify as worthy of further investment. I may decide that a particular piece warrants closer attention and effort in order to prepare it for an audience of readers.

Student writers certainly benefit from having a writing folder. When the time comes to lift a piece from the notebook for further 'development', a folder provides the freedom for writing to spread and expand across several pages, if the writer so desires. The writer has the option to cut and paste and generally move the writing about.

Some teachers encourage student writers to leave a blank page opposite the writing page in their notebooks. The aim here is to allow students the option of adding additional information, changes and the like. This idea works because it is about growing the writing. So, how do we maximise the potential of the writer's notebook? And how do we improve the situation for student writers?

The following actions help to preserve the integrity of the writer's notebook:

- **Increase professional reading about writing.** Books such as Ralph Fletcher's (1996a) *Breathing In, Breathing Out: Keeping A Writer's Notebook*, or Aimee Buckner's (2005) *Notebook Knowhow* provide a great insight into using notebooks. These books provoke thought and provide practical advice on how to launch a writer's notebook in ways based on best practice principles.
- **Increase use of the writer's notebook by teachers.** We learn by doing. For the notebook to be truly impactful, it requires teachers to be willing to embrace it. This requires risk-taking educators willing to lead the way forward for student writers. The notebook is not just another thing we *make* students do. The notebook allows us to share the learning journey. Sharing notebook entries provides the novice writer with further insight into how a notebook might look. Let the sharing begin!
- **Strengthen the reading–writing links.** Embrace literature as a tool for teaching writing. Teachers of writing are never alone. Mentors await discovery. Unwitting collaborators exist in the form of authors we know and trust. Learning to read like a writer is an essential skill for all teachers of writing.
- **Teach students to harvest ideas for writing.** This implies the teacher knows exactly where ideas reside. It requires the most proficient writer in the classroom leading the way by

sharing these places with students. A simple place to start would be books, places, people, pictures, photographs, media, life-events… the world awaits. By illuminating these essential connections, the less experienced writer is alerted to enormous potential for writing. A special kind of energy is released.

- **Allow student choice in the configuration of their notebooks.** One size doesn't fit all! Encourage notebooks of various sizes to suit various situations. Ownership is critical to investment. Differentiation has many applications. The uniqueness of each writer should be reflected in their notebook choices.

- **Use the notebook to make lots of 'starts'** before choosing one special piece that might be lifted out of the notebook and developed further.

- **Develop the notebook as a place for the student writer to experiment, collect, and wonder through writing.** It is vital to mindfully link thinking to writing.

- **Encourage students to fill the pages of their notebooks with words and ideas.** Let them follow your lead as a joyfully literate educator and writer.

CONSIDER

Encourage inexperienced writers to take their notebooks out into the world beyond the walls of the classroom and the school grounds. Be daring. Dare young writers to venture into different spaces and write. Set the notebooks free! Writing in different places provides different perspectives for writing. Show young writers how your own notebook is an instrument of portable magic, a travelling companion. Bring outside influences to the pages of your notebook.

Removing impediments to writing is critical for writing growth. When writing takes off with students, the notebook begins to realise its true potential as a writing resource. Teaching with your notebook as a model represents a clear demonstration of your commitment as both writer and teacher.

13

STARTING OUT WITH YOUR OWN WRITER'S NOTEBOOK

When considering where to begin with writing, a possible starting point is for the teacher to share their own writer's notebook. Naturally, this presupposes that the teacher has realised the importance of being a teacher who writes. Such an understanding makes it easy to be a writer who teaches. In this situation, standing before these impressionable young writers is an authentic model of a writer. Someone to lead the way. Young writers may even use some of the ideas sighted in the teacher's notebook(s) to spark writing ideas of their own. 'What did you notice when you were looking at my notebook?'

Following the sharing of the notebook, a chart or list of possible notebook inclusions might be created, containing many of the following:

- Lingering questions and wonderings
- Memoir pieces
- Opinion pieces
- Descriptions of places, people, events
- Recounts
- Fiction/fact/faction (a blend of fact and fiction) stories

- Poems
- Reviews
- Reports
- Rants and raves
- Lists
- Cut-out pictures, headlines, banners and articles from newspapers and magazines, used to generate writing ideas
- Collected ephemera such as tickets, photographs, brochures and stickers from places that you visit and things that you do
- Maps of favourite places, your route to school, your house, an imaginary land
- Collected memorable quotes to spark your thinking and launch writing ideas
- Sketches, illustrations and doodles from which you 'draw' inspiration
- Writing pieces about family – its traditions, stories and history
- References to favourite places, objects, recipes.

After a few weeks of notebook entries have been completed, conduct a silent share session. Some teachers refer to this as a gallery walk (a walk around the room silently observing and making notes about the great things they are witnessing in the notebooks of fellow writers).

Students each select a page they believe best demonstrates their thinking and documenting as a writer. Leave that page open on a table/desktop and allow others to read, observe and note ideas they believe might assist them to become better writers. Following the silent share, allow time to discuss some of the great ideas seen during the focused gallery walk of the classroom.

Hopefully, these ideas will build content and confidence within your burgeoning community of writers. Remember, though, those notebooks need regular feeding to stay healthy.

For the inexperienced writer, learning to find suitable writing ideas – ideas that allow them to explore matters more deeply – is a skill requiring practice, time and persistence to develop.

For teachers, it remains important to show student writers how to identify potential writing ideas – to show them where ideas can be found – which is basically all around them. We must let them in on this secret hiding place in plain sight. They frequently overlook possibilities purely because they are not practised observers.

Instilling within student writers a belief that the story of their life matters and is worthy of sharing with readers needs to drive teaching efforts. Sharing how a more experienced writer determines what they will write about and how they will present their writing ideas is an important step in developing self-directed, confident and independent writers.

Apart from talking about their lives, young writers should be encouraged to share what they discover from their life experience. These vignettes hold much potential for propelling writing forward. They say much about success and failure, life lessons, and the full gamut of human emotions. The secret lies in getting our young writers talking and sharing.

Encourage student writers to maintain a close connection to their writer's notebook. Make it a travelling companion. Keep it handy and write, draw, paste anything that presents as a possible writing inspiration.

Write about what's closest to the heart: Young writers must understand that they should only write about those things closest to their heart. Writing about matters that need to be expressed, things that should not be forgotten and things that they want the wider world to know all deserve their attention. Writing about topics for which they have no affinity is largely a waste of time and effort. They should write to discover, uncover, explore, share and understand themselves and their world. They should write to express feelings and opinions, to explain, inform and persuade, to describe beauty and ugliness. Writing is as much about the mud as it is about the flowers. A lifetime of possibilities lies there to be discovered.

Create lists of potential writing ideas: Ask student writers to try to list up to ten possible writing topics. Then get them to choose one item from the list and make a second list of ten things associated with the identified topic. Begin by writing about one of the items on the second list. It's about narrowing down the topic, refining the search.

Brainstorming: This is a vital thinking skill. Young writers MUST be allowed to see brainstorming modelled by a more experienced writer in order to appreciate its power to generate potential writing possibilities. Allow them to see how the most proficient writer in the room generates ideas. Demonstrate how you are able to undertake some serious brainstorming, then invite your students to follow your lead. If you do this, you are making the learning visible. Merely telling the inexperienced writer to brainstorm will not cut it. Allow them to reach an understanding that brainstorming is about generating as many ideas as possible in a short amount of time. It is quantity before quality. Once a list of potential ideas has been compiled, then the essential sorting (and possible culling) of those ideas can commence.

Reading: This remains a great way to discover potential writing ideas. What do other writers write about? How do they write about specific topics and themes? What genres do they mostly choose when writing about certain topics? Encourage young writers to explore these questions in order to reveal what it is they truly wish to say as writers.

Observe: Encourage student writers to more effectively engage with their surroundings. Give them cameras or provide them with materials and time for sketching. Discuss the finer detail of these images. Ask them to describe what is just beyond the image. Lock in these observations by encouraging talk and discussion and see where it leads the writers. Link this work to the work of photographers and illustrators.

Collect: Utilise artefacts and ephemera in notebooks as a stimulus for writing.

Rehearsal: It represents a major breakthrough in the development of the student writer when they become conscious of rehearsing their writing ideas. As a classroom teacher, it was cause for celebration for me when students entered the classroom some mornings and announced, 'I know what I'm going to write about today.' It was music to my ears to hear those words. They were telling me that they were conscious of their writing intentions well before the act of writing. They were rehearsing their writing ideas. These young writers were taking their writing beyond the four walls of the classroom and engaging in preparation and thinking about the writing that would eventually emerge on the blank page.

I fully understand how important rehearsal is to the writer. I find myself continually in the grip of word storms. They bounce around in my head. Phrases and ideas form and reform continually as I go about this critical pre-writing phase. I am getting ready to write. I am sorting ideas. I am sounding myself out. *How does this sound? What about if I try this?* This process can take up a significant amount of time. Eventually these ideas will spill onto the page and from there further reshaping takes place.

One of my writing mentors, the late Eric Rolls (1986), writes about this rehearsal phase in his wonderful little book *Celebration of the Senses*:

> From the time I begin to plan a book, phrases sing in my head. I write most of them down at once, stopping the car, the tractor, getting out of bed…
>
> The phrases I like I do not write down. I say them to myself over and over. I say them when I wake up at night. I say them in the morning. I know where the phrase is to fit in the book. I will sing it over and over…

This is how it goes: the recursive nature of rehearsing your words. Wordplay that largely retains its invisibility until it is ready to be revealed on the page. Non-writers will not appreciate this. They will not understand. Young writers deserve to know that rehearsal is a natural part of writing. They need to be encouraged to think about it as part of the pre-writing phase. It is homework in its purist sense. It is homework that actually provides a dividend.

Investigate: Find out how writers write, why they write and how they use notebooks to stimulate the writing lives they lead. Investigate how other writers choose their topics and how they go about the processes of writing. How do they make their writing inviting for others to read? Raise awareness among young writers of the myriad options that confront writers daily.

All these actions will be even more effective if you, the writing teacher – the most proficient writer in the classroom – regularly demonstrate how you go about these very same things when teasing out important ideas for writing.

It Takes Courage to Write

Writing requires courage. For those who have made a conscious decision to write for and with their students, I applaud you! What you are doing is indeed brave. There are many cultural and societal prejudices that obstruct the uptake of writing, thus making it difficult in some communities for writing to flourish. For some, the struggle to write is bound up in the misguided notion that it is somehow not cool to reveal your inner thoughts or commit your personal ideas to paper. As a consequence, the emotional self and the imaginative self are suppressed, discouraged, censored. In many cultures, the struggle to write is aligned with the erroneous belief that particular voices and lives matter little in the literary sense.

For some, writing is difficult because of some pre-existing hang-up dating back to an earlier experience at school (or even home) where harsh and unjustified judgments snuffed out the writing flame. Writing became an assignment that had to be endured in order to placate adult expectations. For many of these people, writing withered and died once the assignments stopped coming. For others, writing during their formative years was associated with pain and suffering. It may have been viewed as something an elite few were able to do.

So, in classrooms where teachers are facing up to the same challenges as their student writers, a significant change is occurring. These changes – these moments of revelation – require a certain amount of risk taking and determination in order for writing to flourish. As Pat Schneider

(2005) states in her book *Writing Alone and With Others*: 'To write is to reveal your mind at work.' For this reason, I say, to write takes courage. If you are a teacher who takes the brave step to make your writing life visible, I have no doubt your students will be impressed and feel supported by your brave actions.

As a writer, I have choices. I understand how important it is for every other writer to have this same critical option. Every writer deserves the same level of choice when it comes to their writing. They need to know what it feels like to think about their writing intentions. The natural response is to feel a desire to act upon such thoughts and ideas. Choice empowers the writer. In classrooms it should begin with allowing student writers to decide what kind of writer's notebook in which they wish to write. Choice should continue to expand from this point on…

It is important to allow students to choose the shape and form of their writer's notebook. Standardisation of notebooks is easy for teachers, but it sends the wrong message regarding choice. It shows a distinct lack of respect to the emerging writer. I choose the notebook that works for me. Student writers should be able to do the same. Notebooks should not look like a string of sausages.

The notebook should be a place to feel safe as a writer. It is a place to experiment, to make discoveries and wonder. It is a place to find your own particular voice.

As Desire, a Grade 5 writer, noted: 'A writer's notebook doesn't have a voice. The words you write in the notebook give it a voice.'

Choice and voice are inextricably linked. The more teachers attempt to control writing and stifle choice, the less likely it is that voice will be in evidence on the page.

When writers are encouraged to find their voices, they begin to write more carefully about their observations and experiences of their immediate world. Choice of subject matter expands. The influence of mentors gains traction. Consequently, they become more likely to align their writing to the passages of writers they admire. They begin to explore a range of emotions connected to particular areas of their lives. As a result, the writing produced edges closer to their subject of choice and is therefore less distant from their readers. They are more likely to explore their own motives and actions. As a student once informed me: 'The more I wrote, the more I remembered.' Thoughts and feelings bubble to the surface and spill across the page. The rise of honest and truthful words becomes more apparent.

As the developing writer grows in confidence, they also become more open to experimentation, a little braver with style, mode and mood. More writing time is requested. When we as writers feel good about our efforts, we feel energised. We want more of that same feeling.

Students who lack voice in their writing often struggle with writing stamina and confidence. They are hesitant in writing even a sentence and are frequently anxious regarding word choice. The writing tends to lack an essential flow. Words dribble onto the page in need of resuscitation.

The challenge of writing is immense if the writer has little practice in composing fluent sentences. They constantly stop and ponder what might come next. They hesitate when confronted with spelling and grammar decisions. They feel overwhelmed by the various demands of composition. This is often characterised as writing reluctance, when in fact it is a confidence issue. These writers want to be able to write fluently, but they lack the necessary experience and self-belief. More time to practise writing (as well as reading) is required, along with regular exposure to writing mentors where exciting word use and exemplars of grammar and punctuation can serve as inspiration.

It surprises me how the approach of many teachers to student writing is so genre specific. It may be neat and painless to teach this way, but it lacks authenticity, and the teacher frequently assumes ownership of the task. I never write merely to practise a specific genre. I am driven by ideas. As Bob Dylan famously wrote in his iconic song 'My Back Pages', I like 'using ideas as my maps'. Writing sometimes is a bit of a messy beast. There is much satisfaction to be gained in learning to bring the beast under control. With time and effort, it evolves into a more ordered thing. Writing is, after all, a problem-solving activity.

When a student approaches me and opens the conversation with a statement like 'I want to write about fishing', my response is, 'How do you see yourself writing about this?' Immediately, we establish in the mind of the young writer the notion of choice. Choice is imperative...

Choice motivates efforts to write, and this in turn builds confidence. Consequently, the desire to stay engaged is heightened. Each day, I anticipate writing. Usually, I have a sea of possibilities surging through my head – topics and issues that have been consuming my conscious thought across previous days and hours.

I recall a memorable conversation with author and illustrator Terry Denton as we stood looking over Fisherman's Beach, Mornington, waiting for our respective children to exit the water. Terry's words have remained with me over the intervening years. He shared his experience of how writing ideas came calling, remarking that they revolve around in his head like clothes in a tumble dryer. They mingle with other ideas. When they're ready, the ideas are taken out, fresh and ready to use. It was a great analogy for the rehearsal writers' experience.

So, I ruminate. I rehearse. I ponder possibilities. This propels me into the writes of the day. I think about the writing idea provoking me the most and ask, 'How do other writers choose to write about this topic/issue? Do I want to follow their lead, or do I want to write about this in another way, another form?'

Essentially, it is a matter of issue before genre, topic before form. I have a raft of choices regarding what to write. The next choice concerns how I might write it. I may choose a particular shape and form for a writing piece, or I may compose a hybrid text that crosses several genres. This is the power of choice!

The questions for me as a writer are:

- What's appropriate for this piece of writing?
- What do I want to achieve?
- Who will be reading this (audience considerations)?

It is at this point my thinking and my notebook merge and the raw words begin to flow. When we share the many truths of our writing lives with students, our teaching can have a profound effect on their writing lives. We encourage the growth of the meta-cognitive writer.

Changing Notebooks

Mixed feelings swirl around me when commencing a new writer's notebook. The prospect of filling the fresh pages brings with it anticipation, a prospect to be enthusiastically embraced. To see newly generated words spread out across previously unmarked pages delivers a buzz. The very act of capturing the raw stuff of my writing life delivers order and a sense of accomplishment to my active mind. The harvesting of words and ideas adds to the energy for writing in this new place. I am like the farmer ploughing a new field.

I make a conscious decision to choose a notebook with different dimensions and qualities to its predecessor. Some writers choose the same notebook each time a replacement is required. I embrace the notion of change. It affords me the unique shape and form of each successive writer's notebook.

I remain keen to shape this new notebook in a way that establishes its difference from previous notebooks. The contents will add further to the individuality. There will be new discoveries. I am keen for my notebooks to possess unique attributes – a bit like people.

This changeover time, however, remains a bittersweet moment in my writing life. I am confronted with saying farewell to a trusted friend. I am saying goodbye to a travelling companion, the willing catcher of my thoughts and dreams. The notebook just completed has been with me every day in the lead-up to the changeover. Everywhere I have been, it has been there too. One rather special notebook travelled home with me from Rome after my wife purchased it there. It was a birthday surprise – a beautifully constructed leather-bound notebook with generously thick pages. I had to wait to use it, as I had just started another notebook at that time. It was like getting a brand-new bike as a Christmas gift and not being allowed to ride it until Easter!

Another notebook (also a gift) represented a stunning departure from any of its predecessors. It was manufactured by Karst, a Sydney-based company that prides itself in producing sustainable products. This notebook was made from recycled, pulverised stone. No tree, water or bleach was used in its production, making its carbon footprint noticeably smaller. It contained pages made from stone, if you can imagine that. The resulting product was smooth and durable. When I pick it up, this particular notebook feels noticeably heavier in my hand and the pages discernibly different to the touch. Like Australian currency notes, the pages possess a somewhat waxy quality when touched. As a result, the ink took longer to dry, the pages being less absorbent. Writing in this notebook represented a slightly different feel, I must say. It was an ideal notebook for Covid lockdown times, as I didn't have to carry it about as much as I would normally do.

During the handover period, when I am transitioning from one notebook to another, I consciously carry both notebooks with me. There exists a natural connection. A connection stretching across time. One notebook informs the other.

I am keen to create a bridge between the old and the new. As my new notebook begins to fill, it will reach a point where it will contain sufficient content to travel solo. The older notebook will be gently retired to become part of my ever-expanding collection of completed notebooks, stretching back to 1983.

My just-completed notebook will continue to play an active role in my writing life. While it will cease to be my travelling companion, I will periodically revisit it and my other notebooks for the purposes of reconnecting and rereading. I am conscious of the vital role rereading plays in informing my writing ideas. It will serve as a source for research and reinvigoration. It is from reading old entries that new ideas frequently reveal themselves. I will adopt the role of treasure hunter and text detective. I will mindfully excavate potential writing gold.

Rereading old notebook entries is akin to a reunion with an old friend. I take great joy and renewed pleasure in such reconnections. These notebooks are central to my existence as a writer and educator. All my published work began a tentative existence within the collective pages of various notebooks. They represent the footprints left by my writing journey, my life's journey.

> The notebook is the place where you figure out what's going on inside you or what's rattling around. And then, the keyboard is the place that you go to tell people about it. (Kleon, 2024)

If you are embracing the writer's notebook for the first time, you may well ask the question 'What types of entries might one gather when starting out?'

I am not a great fan of writing prompts, but if you are having trouble getting inspiration, these ideas might prompt your thinking around what to write. Maybe they will help you to think of a connection to a topic/idea you feel strongly about. Most importantly, I urge you to dive straight in and start filling the pages with your words.

- Write about the first book you remember reading.
- Create a life map to show events in your life so far.
- Write an entry about one of the items on your life map.
- Write an entry about any topic of your choosing.
- Write about your personal opinion.
- Write a response to a book you are currently reading.
- Write about the meaning behind a treasured object – what memories do you associate with that object?
- Create a plan for a memoir piece.
- Write a memoir including all the sensory details.
- Make a list of your personal choosing – e.g., things that take time.
- Persuasive writing – choose an issue that is important to you and write a persuasive piece.
- Write a short narrative about being sick as a child.

- Write about a place you would go right now and why.
- Create a list of things you still wish to do.
- Write about a time when you knew you were in trouble.
- How did you spend your pocket money?
- Create a list of things you never intend to do.
- Write about an embarrassing moment.
- Write about your relationship with weekends.
- Write a list of things you don't need.
- Write about noise.
- Write about silence.
- Write about pretending.
- Make a list of questions you wished you had asked.
- Write about your feet.
- Write about your treasures.
- Write about something you wish you could still do.

New Ideas Exist in Old Notebook Entries

I am forever rereading my notebooks. It enables me to excavate ideas or resurrect lost entries. I build on the slightest glimmer of an idea that may eventually grow into something more significant. Rereading often awakens writing on a new front. New ideas frequently grow out of old notebook entries. This I know from experience.

I captured the following entries in my notebook, some of which came from my habit of rereading. It's a rather eclectic collection of notebook entries. Who knows where they might lead me in the future…

> A factoid: it is illegal to wear a tie in Iran (another example of western decadence, it seems).

> Two cartoons by the great Michael Leunig. His unique observations on political and social issues provide great fodder for thinking and writing.

> A recollection of a Baltimore classroom I visited in 2004. (I dredged up the entry from an earlier notebook. This rereading

of the stuff I've collected enabled me to rediscover something I felt strongly enough to write about in greater detail.)

Another factoid: more tigers are kept in private compounds in the United States than exist in the wild.

The cost of limes in my local supermarket has reached a staggering $1.78 EACH! They look so puny. So much for margarita salvation!

I wrote a piece about the writer as observer.

Some notes regarding the physical environment of the classroom.

I wrote about the glorious arrival of long-overdue rain.

The regular rereading of notebook entries must develop as a habit. Learn to excavate those hidden gems to see if there are any entries capable of sparking ideas for further writing. Frequently, new ideas for writing emerge from older ones.

The Collecting of Essential Snippets

I once suggested to a class of young writers that, if they were looking for writing ideas, they should practise the art of eavesdropping and listen for snatches of conversation that regularly float past – words of wonder that hang in the air, waiting to be rounded up and written down.

A boy looked at me quizzically, before informing me his parents had told him it was impolite to listen in to other people's conversations. I recalled my own collection of parent tapes. A host of ancient messages swirl around in my brain, reminding me that children should not be listening to adult conversations.

I tried to reassure him that, as writers, we enjoy a special exemption, so long as we are tactful when listening. He remained unconvinced.

Poet Naomi Shihab Nye (1996) backed my position on this issue when she wrote:

> I have also kept notebooks of things other people say – even people I don't know, in airports, on trains. Students in lunchroom lines at schools. Sometimes these quotes are very mysterious, or intriguing, and will lead us somewhere else. I have a whole notebook filled with quotes by an old friend of mine named Kerry. When we have trouble thinking of a beginning for a piece of writing, we may struggle to come up with a line from our own minds, an idea. We might be better starting with a line we have heard, letting it be an invitation into a piece.

So, with this endorsement ringing in my ears, I will push ahead with my listening in – my eavesdropping. Writers write with their ears. Mine are tuned to the world around me and remain on alert, ready to receive.

It turns out that even bees eavesdrop. They have learned to save time looking for pollen by avoiding visiting places depleted by other species. They listen in and use pheromones to alert them to such information.

Student writers should be encouraged to add eavesdropping to their ever-increasing writer's armoury. We need to show them how we use it to inform our own writing, so they can make use of it when attempting to employ effective dialogue. My notebooks are full of wondrous sound bites. While going about my daily life, I frequently overhear snatches of interesting and notable conversation. As each new day unfolds, I find myself listening constantly for little snippets of conversation, little word encounters, alive with potential to form part of future writing pieces. I collect them in my notebooks – quotes and conversational titbits ready for sprinkling through writing projects:

> What did you do with that pen I lent you two days ago? *(Source: Café Modi)*

> We used to collect spiders in jars from the different places we visited because our son was doing a project on spiders. How's that for dedication? *(Source: Café Modi)*

> I love you, even if you are a derr-brain! *(Source: Café Modi)*

I like being the boss. If I were in charge of the world, I'd fix things immediately. *(Source: Café Modi)*

My dad used to say, if you touch things in my shed, I'll sneak in while you're asleep and unscrew your belly button and when you wake up in the morning, your bum will drop off. *(Source: school staffroom)*

I don't know why they stock ostrich, I would much prefer buffalo. *(Source: Park Slope Food Co-op shopper)*

I only sell good quality, you look. Raybans only $6! *(Source: Canal Street Market stall)*

What's so romantic about living in a lighthouse? Let me tell you, it's just me and a lot of fish – and I hate fishing! *(Source: Lighthouse keeper in radio interview)*

Keith came into school this morning and announced that his pet snake had died. I could tell he was upset so I allowed him time to compose himself. So he goes to the back of the room, drinks a bottle of that blue juice and then begins throwing things around the room. That blue juice is so chock full of sugar – we're the ones who should be drinking it – then we could keep up with them! *(Source: Teacher)*

Stop your gum thumping! *(Source: Man in street to friend)*

I taught seventh grade for three years and then I realised I wasn't a morning person – AND I didn't like kids! *(Source: Woman overheard in Café Europa, NYC)*

Yummy, yummy. Good for tummy. *(Source: Waiter outside Istanbul Café)*

This is fodder for the writer within. Gathering these valuable snippets is a never-ending project. Listening to voices and snatches of conversation on the subway, on the street and in cafés is the essential stuff of writing. They are stored in my notebook, awaiting deployment. Learn to listen, wherever you go, is pretty sound advice.

CONSIDER

In classrooms where brave teachers dwell, there are signs of genuine progress towards authentic writing practice. In these classes, curious learners are encouraged to write for their own purposes across a range of genres. They are alerted to the craft of writing. Their teachers enlist the support of numerous mentor authors to teach students to write with greater confidence and clarity. Be this teacher...

Curiosity is central to effective teaching. Teachers who exhibit natural curiosity grow professionally. When teachers of writing investigate the effectiveness of their teaching strategies, they become more confident and effective in their teaching.

The challenge is to create a classroom climate in which curiosity thrives, thinking is mindfully cultivated, and the prospect of discovery energises actions for the entire writing community. Young writers in such classrooms are consistently alerted to the importance of becoming keen observers, eavesdropping on the world around them. Ah yes, a word whispered here, an utterance there, and all within the reach of the alert ears of an emerging curious writer.

14

ESTABLISHING OWNERSHIP AND ENGAGEMENT

When writers' notebooks are introduced into classrooms as part of a writing program, it is vitally important that the integrity of the notebook be preserved. How the notebook is perceived by both teachers and students becomes a critical consideration.

It is not the role of the educator to tame the words that enter a young writer's notebook. The notebook should at all times remain a slightly wild place for a writer to work with words. The young writer needs encouragement to roam the literary terrain in search of words and ideas, discoveries and the inspiration to write in that space. It is important to preserve a view of the notebook as a place to explore possibilities. We must convince the inexperienced, through our own actions, that the notebook they own is hungry to receive their words. It needs to be well fed in order to remain healthy. This is an analogy that children readily understand.

Every effort must be made to prevent the writer's notebook from becoming something the teacher feels a need to claim or control. If young writers are to embrace the notebook, ownership must never be wrested away. Conscious encouragement to own the space and be responsible for the words that assemble there must drive teaching. If teachers descend upon the notebooks and the content, it won't take long for the integrity to fizzle and die. The unique status of the notebook will evaporate. Risk taking and experimenting will shrink away, replaced by teacher pleasing and safe writing.

The best way – the only way – to influence a child's view of their notebook is for the teacher to attend to their own notebook. The most powerful declaration a teacher can make regarding the central role a notebook plays in the life of a writer is to regularly share entries with highly impressionable young writers. Such action is the embodiment of the well-known saying 'show, don't tell'. Of equal importance is for teachers to share the processes surrounding the writing they choose to share. It is critical for student writers to know how writing entries are gathered – and why. They need to know where we go for inspiration.

Young writers need to know about the range of writing territories from which writing is collected and added to a more proficient writer's notebook. The impressionable young writer needs to know how reading influences writing. They need to understand what we do to get ready to write. They need to know how we as adult writers deal with writing roadblocks. Allow young writers to witness your problem-solving actions.

A clear statement of intent is made when a more experienced writer shares notebook entries and mindfully discusses their processes for maintaining a writing resource. It is a statement about the valued place the notebook holds in the mind of a more proficient writer.

These mindful actions are a precious gift to impart. They provide an authentic model for the young writer to draw upon, delivering a full measure of confidence and direction to these writers under construction.

Further opportunities arise when teachers share how they use the collected notebook treasure to help launch writing projects. Showing young writers how to lift words from the notebook, into the light, for a wider audience to read is so important. It allows for the sharing of powerful teaching moments.

The aim of all this is to secure the writer's notebook as a valuable writing resource. When writers' notebooks are introduced with such expectations in place, writer agency is tangibly supported. A self-directed, independent writer is more likely to emerge. The notebook is more likely to fulfil its intended purpose. The writer remains engaged; the notebook remains valued. Teaching delivers joy and satisfaction.

Decision Making

Decision making is such a difficult undertaking for some people. I recall a scene in an Indian restaurant in Phuket, Thailand, during a visit in 2008 where a fellow traveller experienced great difficulty arriving at a dining decision.

I was enjoying a meal with my wife, Vicki, and engaging in what can most accurately be described as *people watching*. Studying human behaviour is both fascinating and instructive. It provides great fodder for the writer within. People watching is the ultimate portable pastime…

A woman entered the restaurant, and the waiter immediately seated her at the next table. She then spent almost 15 minutes attempting to place an order from the menu. She remained vigilant in her efforts to avoid 'spicy food'. I wondered if she had merely stumbled into the restaurant, without noticing that it actually specialised in Indian cuisine. She laboriously worked her way through the extensive menu, exhausting the efforts of two waiters, before finally settling on her order.

Displaying admirable patience and understanding, the waiting staff had guided the hesitant diner towards a loose version of decision making. They were a tag team of sorts, changing when the dithering diner slipped into one of her several silent pondering poses. There was to be no spice in her life!

I found myself unable to remain long enough to see if the selections she eventually arrived at met the stringent criteria she had set. I left somewhat dissatisfied with the lack of closure to my observations. As I returned to the bustling street, I was left only to speculate. But I had fun with the possibilities.

Diners must make decisions. Writers too must be prepared to make decisions. At every step of the writing process, the writer encounters metaphorical forks in the road. Decisions, so much a part of living our daily lives, remain equally integral to writing…

Assisting Student Writers to Make Best Use of Their Notebooks

Students frequently need extra guidance and support to develop the essential momentum and confidence for success when writing. At the beginning of a new school year, they are learning to trust a new teacher, new surroundings and new classmates. There is much to consider. It takes time to adapt to new routines and expectations when this new learning partnership is in its formative stages. The student wonders, 'What does this teacher expect of me as a reader and writer?' If it is the teacher's intention that students use a writer's notebook, then it will require mindful leadership aimed at revealing the hidden potential of this writer's resource. Teaching must reveal to the inexperienced learner how a notebook can play an effective role in their daily lives as writers.

Used appropriately, writers' notebooks allow developing writers to make stronger connections to the world and their encounters with life. The harvesting and documenting of their daily lives provides an easy, informal way to start thinking about potential topics and ideas. In time, and with consistent encouragement, the developing student writer learns to become progressively more observant. These experiences lead to increased engagement. With time and practice, the notebook holds the potential to become a purposeful collection zone for a myriad of 'stuff', to stimulate and grow writing.

Embryonic writing ideas, experiments with words, favourite quotes, amazing facts and trivia, lists, dreams, wonderings and ideas for the future begin to spread across the notebook pages. The statement '*I don't know what to write about*' fades like vapour. Uncertainty is replaced by a sense of curiosity and wonderment.

CONSIDER

Before we write for a potential audience, we must learn to derive pleasure in our own work as teachers who write. The writer's notebook becomes crucial is this pursuit. We must be open to showing the less experienced writer how we go about finding potential ideas to write about. Importantly, we must feel a need inside that compels us to write down that observation, thought, story, poem or memory. Our teaching gains impetus when we learn to recognise and share our own process. Let's remove unnatural impediments to writing. Teach into the notebook through our actions as writers and teachers, then watch the writing take off and the notebook realise its true potential as a writer's resource.

15

THE JOURNEY FROM NOTEBOOK ENTRIES TO WRITING PROJECTS

I don't wait for moods. You accomplish nothing if you do that. Your mind must know it has got to get down to work. (Pearl S. Buck, Interview, 1940)

How can we most effectively support young writers in negotiating the gulf between collecting writer's notebook entries and launching into a self-selected writing project? What is the best way to lift the writing into the light in order for it to be shared with a broader audience?

Helping the inexperienced writer avoid becoming trapped in a whirlpool of copious writer's notebook entries that never grow into something more fully developed (via a self-driven writing project) is a critical consideration for teachers of writing. The answer lies in assisting the inexperienced notebook keeper to develop a vision for their writing.

The writer's notebook is a tool for writing. It is not intended for the entries to become trapped within it. The notebook contains many beginnings, and not all of them are destined to be launched beyond the notebook pages, but their presence affords the writer options. The skill lies in identifying and lifting out the pieces that the writer feels have the most potential for developing into something beyond the notebook page. These are pieces they can imagine themselves working on for a longer time – pieces deserving of sustained attention.

In order to be able to exercise this option, young writers must be assisted to develop a level of expertise with respect to their personal writing. Which entries matter most to them?

Regular reading of notebook entries will assist the writer to identify which entries are worthy of further consideration as possible writing projects. All this rereading helps develop a critical lens through which potential projects may be viewed. Rereading can be employed to help the writer mine new writing possibilities from their older words, their earlier entries.

It is at this critical point that the skill of rereading becomes vitally important. Our teaching energy needs to be directed towards embedding rereading as a feature of the writing process every writer can call upon.

- Assist them to reread as they write.
- Assist them to reread after they have written.

It is preferable to reread the writing aloud after it is completed. This allows the writer to hear the words as a reader would experience them. Encourage student writers to conduct this rereading alone, with a pen or pencil in their hand. They can read to the walls and windows of the classroom and make necessary changes as they go. They should be encouraged to do this prior to asking any other writer to read their words. The writer wants the words on the page to flow easily over the tongue. Reading aloud helps with this critical issue. Such action is respectful of the intended reader. By reading their words aloud, the writer is afforded the opportunity to discover whether the writing piece needs revision and editing. Above all, it must make sense to both the writer and the reader, and this is where this important consideration can be assessed.

All these rereading actions grow the capacity of the inexperienced writer to more confidently appraise their own writing. They encourage the growth of reflection and assist the writer to develop a clearer vision of what might be possible. In growing such reflective writers, modelling and demonstration become vital. These impressionable learners need to see their teachers regularly engaging in these same reflective rereading processes.

They benefit from seeing their teachers:

- Reflect upon their own writing processes
- Reflect upon their own decision-making processes
- Sharing their noticing/learning.

In time, and with regular teacher demonstrations, the young writers should be encouraged to begin sharing their own processes, as well as their writing. This important distinction must be made clear.

Strategies to Grow 'Writing Projects'

- Encourage more writing from students (build writing stamina).
- Rewrite a part of a larger text before discussing the impact of the rewrite.
- Consider examples that support your thinking around a topic, or the thinking of a character.
- Do some wondering: why is this piece of writing important to me?
- Brainstorm to gather additional ideas connected to your writing piece.
  - Are there wider connections?
  - Are there connected memories I can include?

Students can be further supported in developing a more metacognitive view of their writing through:

- Peer feedback
- Authors' circles

- Check-in groups
- Writing conferences
- Share-time feedback.

Consider also the power to influence the attitude and actions of young writers through:

- Modelling your own revisions
- Modelling your own brainstorming
- Sharing your own rereading (think aloud).

Demonstrate your own revisions of a piece of writing you have chosen to lift from your writer's notebook:

- Improving leads
- Improving endings
- Improving dialogue
- Adding variety to sentences – length, starting words
- Developing characters/settings/point of view
- Revising at the word level – verbs, adjectives, nouns
- Reviewing tone, mood.

These writing actions further demonstrate for the inexperienced writer how a writer's notebook informs the writing that follows. They reinforce the notion of the notebook as a valuable launching pad for writing. The notebook becomes more than a repository for their writing ideas. It is not the end, but rather the beginning of something much more significant and powerful. The words contained in the notebook can experience a life beyond the collection zone.

Personal writing projects provide the inexperienced writer with the opportunity to make some genuine, meaningful choices. They become the embodiment of 'Writers make decisions'.

The writer chooses:

- Their own topic/issue
- Their own genre

- Their own purpose
- Their own process
- Their target audience.

They are gifted an opportunity to write in their own way, driven by their own goals and intentions. The chosen project benefits from replicating processes writers employ in the wider world. That way, the project becomes grounded in authentic purposes.

It is important to note that a personal writing project does not equate with the allocation of 'free writing time', where the writer is given a small portion of time to write 'creatively' in the mistaken belief that this provides sufficient investment in supporting and engaging young writers. Such an approach pushes personal writing to the edges of the curriculum in terms of its importance. Such an approach is tokenistic, offering little sense of genuine agency for the developing writer.

In consultation with a more experienced writer – their teacher – the young writer identifies and negotiates the length of the project. Days? Weeks? A term? This brings into play the reality of progression points and deadlines and the use of check-in groups to monitor progress and provide targeted support.

It is important not to lose sight of the distant goal. If the student writer retains a clear vision of where they are heading with the project, it increases the likelihood they will seek out and accept writing advice during conferencing. Allowing young writers this sense of agency does not mean accountability is reduced in importance. The writer is held accountable for the choices they make, and the teacher must work to support the writer to achieve their individual writing goals. During a personal writing project, the teacher is charged with nudging the developing writer to bolster their capacity for self-regulation.

The provision of adequate writing time and resources needs to be factored into the writing workshop sessions. It is not unreasonable to discuss how some of the writing may take place in settings beyond the classroom in order to reach a successful outcome. Writing in different settings challenges the myth that writing only happens in school.

Each writing session should be seen as an opportunity for the young writer to identify process goals for that session. Articulating their intentions makes it more likely the actions will take place and the project will move forward as expected.

Personal writing projects are an important component within a writing curriculum. They deserve equal status and value as that accorded class writing projects. They provide an opportunity to enhance writing relationships. The inexperienced writer learns to problem-solve as a writer, develop craft skills and internalise process skills. Such understandings become part of that writer's armoury.

When the starting point for writing is to commence with what children know, have personally experienced, heard, witnessed, read, or are keenly interested in, motivation and investment can be harnessed in ways that make the project more likely to succeed. The writer is more likely to care. Engagement and persistence become more evident.

The majority of inexperienced writers charge ahead with drafting their writing once they have identified a personal writing project. Experienced writers rarely start with drafting. They frequently invest time in getting ready to write. A significant amount of rehearsal may take place.

For young writers to envision how writing works, they need to be able to see how authors engage in a range of writing-related actions, beyond actual writing. These pre-writing strategies are critical to the eventual outcome of the writing project. Such processes are not bound by age or genre. Young writers are capable of doing these things too.

What writers may do to prepare for their writing project:

- Take photographs of the subject or theme
- Visit a library to research
- Research using the internet
- Research through personal reading

- Reread older writers' notebook entries as research
- Visit a museum or a place of significance
- Interview someone with related knowledge
- Find out more about a particular culture
- Record a conversation with an expert
- Imagine being a particular character in different situations and locations
- Gather related artefacts/ephemera
- Read books on the chosen topic, time period or person
- Read different texts to discover how they want to write about the subject
- Talk to other writers, make notes
- Visit a setting with connections to the project
- Gather opinions
- Make lists of ideas, memories, potential titles
- Write/ask questions
- Draw to clarify and visualise ideas and concepts.

Some questions that might be posed:

- Who could you talk to in relation to this writing project?
- What could you read that is similar to what you wish to write?
- Where could you go to find out more about your chosen topic?
- What could you collect to assist you to be successful in this project?
- What did the writer need to know in order to write this book?
- What do you think the writer might have done before they started to write?
- Where do think the author got the idea for this book/poem/article?
- What do think we would see in the author's own notebook?

A successful writing project needs some time devoted to rehearsing, researching, gathering, thinking and then doing the writing. These actions assist the writer to develop a clear vision of where they want their project to end up. A writing project needs to honour the critical role pre-writing strategies play in moving the writing towards a successful outcome.

The young writer needs to come to an understanding regarding the way a writer's notebook helps the writing grow. Teachers can support children in their pursuit of personal writing projects through the mindful quarantining of daily sustained writing time and the following mindful actions:

- Teaching craft and process lessons
- Sharing how you, as a more experienced writer, generate writing ideas
- Teaching text structures and features of genres in the reading workshop
- Sharing your writing and your own writing process
- Sharing how your writer's notebook informs your own writing projects
- Highlighting a variety of publishing possibilities
- Conferring with writers and offering advice and assistance with goal setting.

When these actions are modelled for students, they are witnessing another writer's commitment to a project. They are learning about persistence and stickability. They are learning to take specific action to realise predetermined goals. Great writing lessons. Great lessons for life.

When I complete a personal writing project, whether it is short or long and complex, I find myself visited by a sense of restlessness. My mind is in fact energised, not tired. I'm thinking, 'What next? Where next?' I suspect the energy arises from the successful completion of the challenge I have set myself. Being successful with a task brings inner satisfaction.

CONSIDER

The challenge is to assist young writers in seeing the value of this type of writing investment. Let's challenge the notion that the first logical action after identifying a potential writing project is to always start writing. For generations, schools have reinforced this approach. It does writers a disservice.

If you still need convincing with regard to the value of personal writing projects, a number of writing studies reveal that better learning outcomes were achieved when children were engaged in self-chosen writing projects, as opposed to writing tasks regulated by others (Brophy, 2008; Garrett & Moltzen, 2011).

16

THE AVENUE OF AGENCY

> Agency is about having control over your choice of writing topic and ownership over how you go about writing it. Agency helps create a culture of writers with self-determination. *(Ross Young & Felicity Ferguson, Real-World Writers: A Handbook for Teaching Writing with 7–11 Year Olds, 2020)*

Across the years, I have worked with many teachers who constantly strove to provide young writers in their care with a genuine sense of agency. They worked respectfully to develop a classroom culture where every writer was encouraged and supported to make informed decisions regarding writing projects they wished to pursue. Many of these teachers were operating from this position before the term agency ever came into vogue.

Agency produces great results. Its presence leads to the successful production of meaningful writing pieces. Writers with a strong sense of agency frequently exceed expectations, improve their academic outcomes and exhibit increased engagement and motivation for writing. They are writers who are more likely to persist. They are imbued with 'stickability'. These writers tend to display greater satisfaction with their written efforts.

If we want to have young writers believing they can act on their own writing intentions, make informed decisions and take suitable actions to reach an identified goal, then our interactions with them need to reflect a sense of a shared vision.

When writers are afforded freedom to choose writing subjects and structures in which they have interest and knowledge, their writing pieces exhibit enhanced organisation, logic and accomplishment.

It is also interesting to note the findings of Fletcher (2016) who found that children with agency pursuing self-selected writing projects are not only more highly committed to completion, but are more likely to seek and accept advice from a teacher during conferencing conversations.

When a teacher helps to instil a sense of agency through their words and actions, it has a positive bearing on learning outcomes. Research further indicates that having a sense of agency improves the performance of low-achieving writers in particular. This has been borne out in research by Peter Johnston (2004).

While agency is vital in developing a positive view of oneself as a writer, it does not guarantee the emerging writer will derive genuine pleasure from writing.

The young writer needs to be provided with regular, mindful instruction in order to use their agency in ways that contribute to meaningful writing development across time.

It is therefore critically important that agency sits comfortably alongside mindful instruction – instruction providing support for the writer's self-efficacy and self-regulation. The teacher must play an active role in teaching the young writer how to write and how to understand and negotiate the processes of writing.

One of the best ways for a teacher/writer to do this is to model and demonstrate aspects of one's own writing process. The young writer is given explicit instruction in a range of craft strategies and techniques they can employ to impact their writing. In this scenario, agency and instruction are presented as essential partners. While agency is a vital component in ensuring engagement and improved performance, it benefits greatly from the partnership with focused instruction on how to write.

As part of this approach, the teacher works with the writer to help establish agreed writing goals. As young writers gain experience, they begin to better understand their own personal writing processes and how certain strategies work best for them. They begin to envisage the writing task as achievable. This self-awareness allows the less experienced writer to successfully complete a writing project they have chosen to undertake.

The end result of all this is that the nurturing of agency coupled with powerful instruction teaches young writers how to develop control over their writing and its accompanying processes. In classrooms where this approach is the driving force for teaching writing, young writers will be more inclined to take writing risks and more likely to write with honesty about topics and ideas meaningful to them. Now, that's an outcome worth a teacher/writer's time and energy.

When writers' notebooks are introduced into classrooms as part of a writing program, it is vitally important that the integrity of the notebook be honoured. How the notebook is perceived by both teachers and students becomes a critical consideration.

If young writers are to embrace the notebook as part of their sense of agency, ownership must never be wrested from them. Conscious encouragement to own the space and be responsible for the words that assemble there must drive the work of the teacher.

The best way – the only way – to influence a child's view of their notebook is for a teacher to attend to their own notebook. The most powerful declaration a teacher can make regarding the central role a notebook plays in the life of a writer is to regularly share entries with highly impressionable young writers. Become the embodiment of the well-known saying 'show, don't tell'.

A clear statement of intent is made when a more experienced writer shares notebook entries and mindfully discusses their process for maintaining a notebook. Highlight the valued place the notebook holds in the mind of a more proficient writer. Then, unpack the back story of how the writing came into existence.

When teachers bring their own writers' notebooks to the attention of less experienced writers, a unique opportunity to demonstrate how and where ideas and inspiration are found and collected emerges. This is such a precious gift to impart. This harvesting of potential writing ideas provides a first-hand model for the young writer to draw upon. It delivers a full measure of confidence and direction. The experienced writer shines a bright light on the power arising from using the notebook as a valued resource. When teachers deep-dive into writing processes and demonstrate how the writing journey might unfold, the developing agentic writer has an all-important writing roadmap to follow – a roadmap consciously highlighted by a more proficient writer. The influence of a teacher/writer is used to positive effect.

I recall a conversation I had with an experienced teacher I had been working with at a school in Melbourne for some time. She informed me that, since committing to writing alongside her Year 6 students, her teaching was delivering much greater satisfaction. She was approaching her teaching with renewed enthusiasm and purpose. 'I am now a learning partner,' she told me. By reimagining her teaching position in relation to how she taught writing, she found herself comfortably located alongside her students as a fellow writer. Agency was being accessed by all members of that classroom community.

Further opportunities arise when teachers share how they use the collected notebook treasure to launch writing projects. Showing young writers how to lift words from the notebook, into the light, for a wider audience to read, is so important. It is powerful teaching without a doubt.

This way, agency, self-efficacy and self-regulation begin working in sweet synchronicity. The relationship between these elements is strengthened. The young writer is supported to manage their individual writing life. They begin to see the actual process they must embark upon to successfully approach writing in a meaningful way. The writer's belief in their own agency is fully realised through such mindful actions. Let's not forget, agency requires the company of intention for writers to fully realise their dreams.

CONSIDER

Promoting writing ownership helps ground the writer's notebook as a valuable writing resource. When writers' notebooks are introduced with these considerations firmly in the forefront of planning, the agency of the writer is tangibly supported. A self-directed, independent writer is more likely to emerge. Importantly, the notebook is more likely to fulfil its intended purpose. The writer remains engaged; the notebook remains valued and healthy. A strong sense of agency develops. The growth of writing agency is actually your superpower as a teacher, because the more you empower your student writers, the more empowered you become as an influential educator.

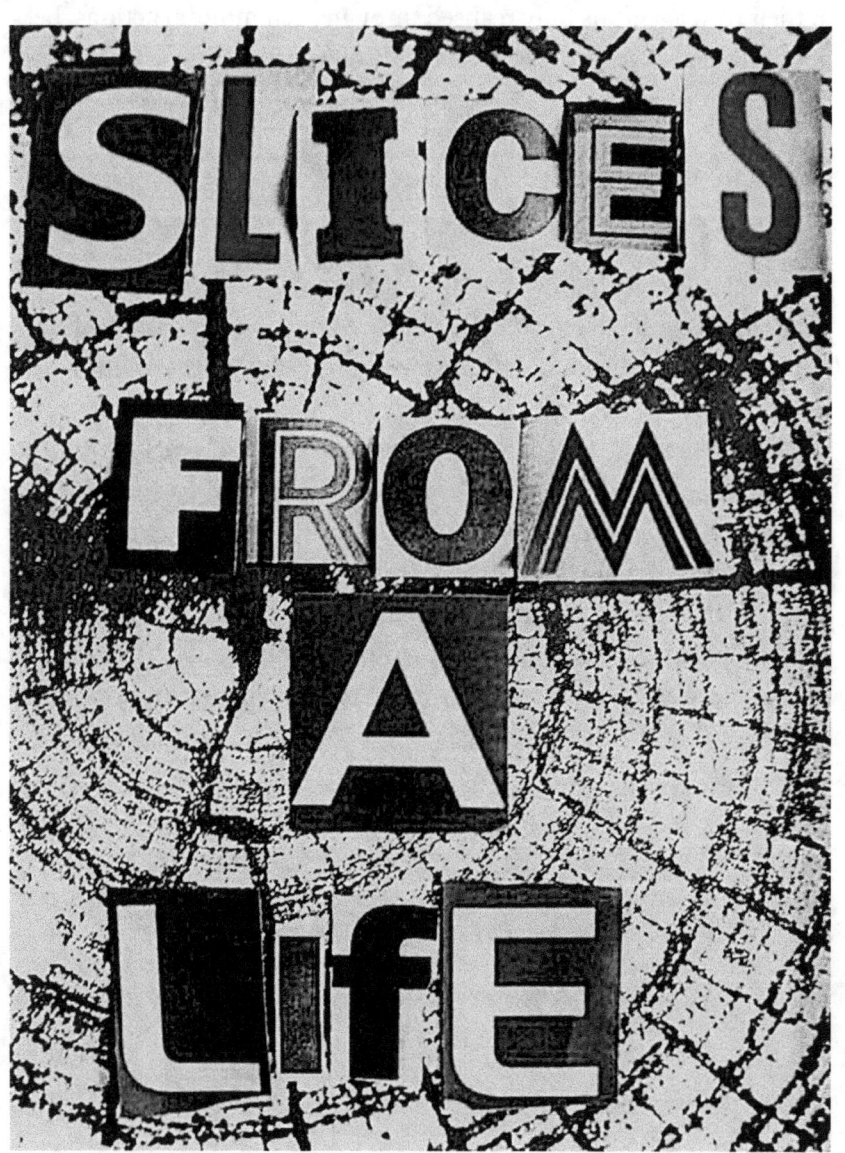

17

SLICES FROM A LIFE

Many entries in my notebooks start out as slices of life. Observations and realisations come rushing at me as I negotiate my various worlds. I capture them in my notebook, and those that make the cut eventually become part of longer pieces for publishing. Some pieces may be incorporated into other writing pieces. I may use just a fragment of the original piece. These slices are essentially fleeting parts of an entire day. Sometimes, I am trying to capture the essence of a small, yet significant (to me) event that drifts within range of my senses.

I become focused on a small moment in time, a scenario maybe. It's using the eye like one would use a camera. The writer within is striving to capture certain images on the page. This approach to writing initially provides insight for me, the writer, and eventually (I hope) for my reader.

My notebooks are littered with such entries. My mind is filled with words before and during the writing. I roll them around in my mind before they spill across the page. Here is a sampling across a range of genres that have been lifted from various notebooks. I also provide the back story for the piece. Maybe these entries will spark possibilities for your own writing; after all, reading is a most worthy pre-writing strategy.

Following Father

I was sitting on the beach one summer, not long ago, when this brief scene took place right in front of me. In the totality of a summer's day, it was an almost negligible moment in time. But my eye caught it, my mind read it and my heart loved it, so it endured. It is but a few brief lines, but as a writer, it pleases me that my notebook trapped it.

> I watch as a young father walks in the damp sand close to the shoreline. His young son follows closely behind. He stretches to place his feet within his father's substantial footprints. This scene is a strong metaphor for father and son relationships. It also prompts me to think of the role of the teacher in the classroom – leading so that others may follow in the teacher's steps…

Incident on the Subway Stairs

During my almost six years living and working in New York, I regularly travelled on the subway system. These experiences provided a rich vein of stories and recollections. I recall, among my many trips, one particular occasion at Essex Street subway interchange. I was walking up the stairs when a small girl, perhaps six years old, and her mother approached from the opposite direction.

> As a mother and daughter descend the stairs down into the subway, I notice that the girl has her eyes tightly closed. Her mother holds the girl's right hand for support as they manage the steps. At first it appears the child is sleepwalking. Then it occurs to me that she has closed her eyes to experience the sensation of walking down the stairs unsighted. She is experimenting. The fact that she has her mother's support gives her the confidence

to take a step into the unknown. At that moment she becomes a risk taker – attempting something new and different…

This brief scene reminded me of the responsibility a teacher faces each time he or she enters a classroom: supporting students to try new and different things, to become risk takers, to think, and dream and above all succeed. It's part of the journey towards becoming an independent, self-directed learner.

Close your eyes for a moment and consider what is possible with the right amount of support. You and your students may take that vital step to discovering your true potential as learners.

The Whistler

Brooklyn, New York, in the depths of winter. It was a brief, yet memorable encounter that compelled me to write. It was one of those experiences you never want to forget. This eventually became a longer, more detailed piece. My initial notebook entry provided a seed for something more expansive.

> Simple moments in our lives frequently turn out to be our greatest pleasures, and so it was just prior to Christmas while standing at a bus stop on an icy and uninviting corner of Vanderbilt Avenue where it crosses De Kalb in Brooklyn's Clinton Hill.
>
> At that precise moment, I had a brief image flash across my mind of my Australian home on Victoria's Mornington Peninsula and dreamed of the warmth of summer in the great southern land. I imagined myself walking along Mills Beach, where I could see brightly coloured bathing sheds – a kaleidoscope of colours fronting the soft expanse of sand. Bathing sheds, beach and sunshine vanished in an instant.
>
> That forlorn Brooklyn bus stop situated directly opposite a funeral parlour added to the grief of this particular street scene. The winter trees lining the street stood as solemn, stick sentinels, their summer glory long past – a leaf-free zone. The walls of

the shops were scarred with generational graffiti, the faded backdrop. A dead umbrella lay in the gutter, and discarded fried chicken bones lay abandoned on the pavement.

The wind blew up the street and slapped me squarely in the face. The bus shelter offered little respite from its icy blasts. I was too cold to bother reading the advertising hoarding. And anyway, it hadn't changed for months. I wrapped my coat more tightly around me, sank down into my scarf and jammed my gloved hands into my coat pockets. I felt no warmer for these efforts. Winter is frequently a bully. Above the swirling wind, the traffic growled as cars and trucks crawled and moaned through the intersection.

I stood in this miserable place alongside three women. No one spoke. On this particular winter's day, no one was wasting their meagre warmth on strangers. We all stood in silence, bracing ourselves against the bitterness of the day. I was counting down the freezing minutes, willing the bus to arrive. I was hoping it would arrive minus the madness that frequently accompanies the middle school students, who clamber aboard each afternoon and swarm, as only social terrorists can. They claim the space with a loud, intrusive hullabaloo. They make travelling on the number 69 bus an ordeal at best. At other times, they make it seem like hell on wheels. On one occasion the bus arrived with the emergency window partially dislodged and screams and wailing emanating from inside. The sound would have scared a banshee. I made a strategic decision to wait for the next bus, in the hope that it couldn't be worse than what this ride offered. I hoped today's bus ride would be less manic.

… And then I heard it. Faintly at first, but discernible as whistling. Where was it coming from, this sweet sound in such a forlorn place? It floated above winter's collective misery. it was coming from somewhere behind me. I turned to see a tall, gaunt man. He was leaning against the wall of a corner deli, directly behind the bus shelter. A bag slung over his shoulder gave me the impression he was journeying home from a day of work somewhere. He wore a cap made of a stocking-type material and a coat that appeared no match for the demands of the day. His whiskery face had a grey sheen, its narrowness reminiscent of the legendary Popeye. I kept taking momentary glimpses, not wishing to lock onto his gaze for fear of making him feel conspicuous, uncomfortable.

The sound of his whistling rose gently above the wind, the traffic and the surrounding ugliness. It spiralled around me. Embraced my consciousness. He was whistling the sounds of the season. 'Let heaven and angels sing.'

I had never heard whistling like this. This man's whistling made a nightingale appear raucous. The rawness of the day was overtaken by the lyrical sound of his whistling. I stood silently, listening to this stranger, and found myself successfully shutting winter out. I wondered if the other people were as absorbed as I was at that moment by one man's whistling… 'Do you hear what I hear?' If the beauty of the whistler's notes were reaching their hearts, their faces failed to reveal their inner joy. They stood like Easter Island statues throughout the entire performance.

The bus arrived just as he launched into 'Deck the Halls'. We all eagerly climbed on board. I stood back so that I could get a better look at the whistling man, as he boarded the bus. The bus was mercifully devoid of crazies, and we all sat in relative peace. I sat opposite the whistling stranger and wondered, 'How have you learned to whistle with such virtuosity? What made you decide to whistle Christmas carols in that drab and depressing place?' I'm glad he did, of course, but it was an unexpected delight. I had approached that bus stop contemplating a battle with winter's freeze and middle school mayhem. I had been moved by one man's attitude to life. The simple act of one man's whistling had refocused my energies.

As I departed the bus near Grand Army Plaza, I passed by the whistling stranger and placed my hand on his shoulder. I thanked him for his beautiful whistling. 'Thank you, sir,' he replied. 'Thank you so much.' He offered me the bonus of a smile.

As we went our respective ways, I felt warmed, and so glad I had made the effort to speak to him. It would have been easy to sit in my seat, wrapped in silence, but then he would never have known what pleasure his whistling had provided. Hopefully, he will continue to whistle, and others will enjoy the simple pleasure I enjoyed. Music is all around us just waiting to be heard. Sometimes you hear it in the most unlikely settings.

The Mystery of the Missing Olives

The mystery surrounding this life episode drove the creation of this short piece. When olives went missing from my solitary olive tree, I was both mortified and mystified. I felt the writer within should be able to make use of this real-life mystery. A mystery taking place on my doorstep – well, not far from it!

> In our front garden stands a single olive tree that was planted more than a decade ago. From the outset, it has been a prolific provider of olives. Interestingly, for the past three years, someone has arrived in the dark of night and harvested the entire crop of olives. We have been shocked to discover our favourite olive tree devoid of olives. Whoever is perpetrating this nefarious act is meticulous – as well as sneaky. Not a single olive is left behind, whether on the tree or on the ground surrounding the tree. It is a continuing mystery, a conundrum of puzzling proportions.
>
> I have made enquiries with an Italian friend of mine, an olive expert, in the hope of finding a solution. I thought maybe the curse of Strega Nona might be able to be invoked. My friend suggested hanging an evil eye ornament in the tree as a deterrent to any would-be olive-nappers. Close circuit video for a single

olive tree may be considered a tad extreme, and sleeping under the tree in June in the Australian winter is a health hazard. Naturally, I remained perplexed by this continuing theft.

At present the tree shows the beginnings of another bountiful harvest. Small green olives hang in abundance from its branches. Come late June they will be black, plump and ready for harvesting. The process of curing them should begin. I am full of anticipation. I am watchful. I am on olive alert.

Postscript: Following my friend's advice, we eventually hung the evil eye ornament among the olive branches, and miraculously the olives remained intact. Now, I am not a superstitious person, but it worked. Maybe the olive snatcher held a fear for such notions. Anyway, the problem was resolved. The identity of the perpetrator of the earlier olive-swiping remains unresolved. It remains an open case as far as I'm concerned.

People-Watching in Mooloolaba

Sometimes, a person enters your life who has an immediate impact. The encounter may be brief but unforgettable. A real character who cries out: 'Okay, describe me, I dare you!' Breakfast in a public place increases the chances of meeting such individuals. The writer must be ready. Observe, but don't stare. Make notes for the brain and salivate at the richness of the scene unfolding before you.

A veteran vacationer approaches the Kool Breeze café. He is adorned in olive-green Bermuda shorts, a pair of matching braces and a Hawaiian shirt that screams 'MISMATCH!' He is hardly inconspicuous, but it matters little, it seems.

He carries an oversized ghetto blaster, grey and gargantuan, under his arm. The man, like the object he is carrying, is large. His stomach is swollen. The belt around his shorts strains in its role of containment. He sports a large head of unruly grey hair, swept back. A full beard, closely cropped, is neat and groomed.

Shuffling in the direction of a vacant table at the front of the café, he is clearly on a mission. Instrumental tones drift incongruously from the ghetto blaster as he approaches his table of choice. He carefully positions the mammoth music-maker on the table. Several adjustments are made to the condiments on the table. Salt, pepper and table menu are all repositioned to make way for the music machine.

At this point, the man slowly wanders to his car, returning with a CD to replace the one currently playing. He presses play with deliberate ceremony, listens closely, pressing forward, before settling into a director's chair to enjoy his selection. Almost instantly, he jerks himself free of the chair. Something appears to be troubling him. He exchanges the chair for a moulded plastic one without arm rests. He settles once more.

By now, every other customer in the café is closely observing the big man's movements – some furtively, others with wide-eyed disbelief.

The soundtrack of his performance pulsates through the morning air. He orders the 'Big Aussie Breakfast' and no one is surprised. 'Eye of the Tiger' bursts forth with the same impact as a fart in a cathedral. A man and his music leave their mark on the morning.

Bizarro World Visitor

Another people-watching experience took place a world away from sunny Mooloolaba. I was travelling on a bus in Brooklyn's Fort Greene area when I encountered an amazing little man…

> At the risk of sounding like I am beginning to lose my tenuous hold on reality, the longer I live in New York, the more I believe in the existence of conspiracy theories. I am increasingly of the opinion that some perverse being from a parallel wacky world keeps sending individuals through a time portal to

manifest themselves in my everyday life. These individuals, whilst generally harmless, have a definite leaning towards the fruitcake category. These half-baked people crop up regularly in the course of my travels around this amazing city. I am yet to work out why.

Before you dismiss me, I invite you to recall Jerry Seinfeld's 'Bizarro World', where everything was the opposite of what you knew. And where was that centred? New York, of course!

To support my theory, I cite WE #327 (That's Wacky Experience number 327), which I had on the No 38 bus whilst travelling down DeKalb Avenue in Brooklyn's Fort Greene area one workday afternoon.

I entered the bus and nonchalantly sat down. When I looked up, there directly opposite me sat a small, elderly man. The first thing I noticed was his seemingly well-tended grey beard, symmetrical in shape and as lovingly tended as a manicured lawn. He was seated adjacent to the front exit. He was almost gnome-like in stature, but this was not what boggled my eyes. It was his travelling outfit. He wore a turquoise tracksuit of dazzling intensity. Over this, he wore a pair of loose-fitting, lime-green shorts. The legs of his tracksuit were tucked neatly into a pair of matching lime-green socks pulled up to calf height. He wore a lime-green woollen cap with a small, red, flashing light smack dab in the centre of it. He also wore a bright-yellow mask pulled up onto his forehead. It reminded me of the type of mask one associates with masquerade balls. On his knees, he wore large, black kneepads, not unlike the kind worn by a small minority of skateboarders, or old floor-tilers with arthritic knees. Around his shins, he wore two larger flashing red lights. They were the kind one more frequently sees on the back of a bicycle. His feet were resplendent in neat black slippers with silver zippers. As he sat there, flashing on and off, his little eyes darted left, then right. I began to speculate on what he might be contemplating.

My first thought was that he might be an ultra safety-conscious cyclist in search of a conveyance. But why the yellow mask?

A young woman securely wrapped in a winter coat and hat boarded the bus and squeezed into the last available seat on the bus. Ironically, it happened to be right next to the small flashing man. Her immediate response was to stare straight ahead of her. She wore a hat that almost covered her eyes, and as she reached up to push it further back on her head, she began to become aware of the living, breathing colour chart seated beside her. She snuck a furtive glance at his flashing shins and then discreetly moved her eyes towards his flashing cap. She then turned her face away like a naughty child. The look on her bemused face said it all.

When the bus stopped outside Fort Greene Park, the focus of our attention was quite literally gone in a flash – down the steps and on his way. We who remained on board were left to wonder about the strangely attired visitor seemingly from another time and place.

Later that week, I was talking to my friend Michael Collins about my latest sightings. I told him of my bus encounter with the strange little man adorned in gaudy colours and flashing lights. Michael immediately replied, 'I know the guy you're talking about! When we lived in St Felix Street, he used to do laps of our block.'

'On a bike?' I enquired, keen to confirm my theory.

'No, he just used to walk or dance his way along the street.'

Then Michael described in perfect detail the outfit I had seen the man wearing on the bus. Hmm, a visitor from a parallel universe, I thought to myself. A unique individual moving to the beat of his own drum and adding colour and delight to my day.

I wonder who will visit me next…

The Great Potato Heist

Writers are storytellers. We sometimes tell our stories many times over before we commit to the act of writing them down. So it was with the following memoir piece. I enjoy telling it as a story because of its very personal connection and the life lessons it conveys. Writing becomes more personal when the topic or focus of the writing is limited to a specific moment in time. The closer the writer can get to a small moment, the more the writing is likely to come to life for the reader; a sense of storytelling emerges for the reader. This memoir piece is my attempt to get close to the moment.

> When a boy is only nine years old, he can do strange things. This was a time when a field of potatoes caused me loads of trouble…
>
> My friend Robert and I decided to take our billycart with us as we set off to explore the local neighbourhood. We were hoping to find a half-decent hill to descend. The billycart had been the product of the previous weekend's efforts. It was strung together using a mixture of scrounged odds and ends. A lettuce box atop a wooden frame, a set of disused pram wheels, and a piece of rope nailed to the front for steering purposes made up this rickety downhill racer. The only modification to the lettuce box was to knock the front panel out so the driver could extend their legs forward to help steer the cart on its wild descent. No brakes, and the lettuce box carriage was so rough that it guaranteed to give you splinters almost every time some part of your body made contact.
>
> We wandered past Les Blake's house, but he wasn't home, so we pressed on towards Boundary Road. We then pushed our way past Mr Porter's horse paddock, towards the great expanse of market gardens. A forlorn-looking brown and white Clydesdale hung its enormous head over the fence and snorted a greeting. We jumped at the sudden appearance of the huge snorting head. Snot dripped from its nostrils, and huge hairs sprouted in different directions from the tip of its long nose. Horse snorts

continued to fill the air as we settled ourselves in the presence of the giant horse.

Clydesdales were rarely seen working the paddocks anymore. This accounted for their sad appearance. They weren't needed, and somehow they knew it. They remained a curiosity, though. We rarely rode past without stopping to pat the gentle giants.

A huge crop of potatoes planted in a paddock beside the horse stable grabbed our attention. They made quite an impressive sight, with their mass of yellow and white potato flowers contrasting with the plain green potato plant leaves. Away in the distance stood a paling fence, forming the border of the constantly advancing houses.

Market gardens like Mr Porter's were being squeezed out as the neighbourhood took on a new appearance. They found themselves surrounded by homes, as new streets were drawn in and new houses constructed. These new houses seemed to appear almost overnight, and the market gardens looked more and more like an endangered species.

Some of the rows near the road had been unearthed, and the potatoes lay exposed on the soil. The rising sun had crusted the sandy soil on their skins. There were potatoes of varying sizes. Fresh, new potatoes, with thin skins. Tiny chats, no bigger than marbles. It was love at first sight for both of us. I could barely contain myself. I saw images of potato heaven. My mind was filled with visions of potatoes chipped, boiled, baked and mashed, with lashings of melted butter. 'Looks like someone forgot to pick up those potatoes,' said Robert, interrupting my potato dreams.

Without another spoken word, we both snuck a glimpse. A full turn of the head revealed not one living soul, save the two of us. It was just two boys, a billycart and a patch of apparently deserted potatoes. It was at this precise moment that good judgment and all the parent tapes that normally looped around in our heads, telling us to do the right thing, left us stranded in the dark zone.

'Let's just take a few,' I said. 'We could cook chips for lunch!'

Robert maintained his silence. He immediately stepped closer to the potatoes. Picking up a handful and clutching them to his chest, he walked back to the billycart and tipped them into the cart where the driver normally sat. I followed like the sorcerer's apprentice, step for step.

We were actually potato-napping, but at that precise moment both of us had our consciences switched off. The billycart filled quickly, and away we scampered, neither quite sure what we were going to do with the loot. That would come later.

'Let's go to your place,' said Robert eventually.

'Why?'

'Oh well, we could cook chips.'

'We've got enough potatoes to cook a mountain of chips. Maybe we'll think of a good idea while we're cutting them up.'

'So, we're going to your place then?'

'S'pose so,' I added reluctantly.

We eventually arrived at my place and pushed the billycart down the driveway that ran beside the house, before entering the backyard. While Robert began cleaning the loot, I slipped inside to get a knife to chop the potatoes into chips.

My mother was ironing and singing when I entered the house. The air was thick with starch, the hiss of steam and Mum's enthusiastic singing. She often sang when she did the ironing. In fact, she was the only person I knew who actually seemed to enjoy ironing. As she sprinkled the clothes with a mixture of starch and water to make them extra stiff, the hissing of the iron provided an accompaniment to her singing. She sang joyfully like the birds of the morning: 'Mares eat oats and does eat oats and little lambs eat ivy. A kid'll eat ivy too, wouldn't you?'

'What have you been doing, my darling boy?' my mother enquired in a matter-of-fact voice. The iron continued to hiss in her hand. Even as she spoke, her eyes never lifted from her ironing board task.

'Not much,' I said, trying to sound offhand.

I was now relying on a voice I used when I had no wish for people to ask questions. My mother knew this voice well. Superior wisdom that only comes from living alerted her to the fact that she needed to do something immediately – like ask more questions.

The sound of someone knocking on the front door distracted her before she could make further enquiries. It seemed that someone was looking for me. I dived my hand into the kitchen drawer, snatched a knife and a vegetable peeler, and then lingered momentarily at the back door. I was curious to know who had saved me from my mother's potentially embarrassing questions. Questions that usually made me blush and squirm and feel strangely hot.

To my absolute horror, the voice at the front door introduced itself to my mother as Mr Porter. I didn't need to hear the rest. Instantly my mind zoomed to the panic zone. I bolted from the house and squealed at the unsuspecting Robert something like: 'Mr Potato is here about the... Porter must have seen us... He's talking to my mum. Hide the spuds quick!'

'What?'

'Come on, get rid of the potatoes!'

'Sure. Where? Up my jumper?'

'Very funny. Come on, think.'

Robert stood before me, his head turning left and right like a carnival clown. His mouth remained agape. He uttered not a single sound.

I suddenly had what I thought was a great idea and without hesitating shared it.

'Chuck the lot!' I spluttered.

'Where?' said my uninspired accomplice. He then resumed his clown pose. Robert obviously needed more information.

'Anywhere,' I said.

'What does that mean? Anywhere!'

'Anywhere, anywhere. Just get rid of them. Chuck them anywhere.'

We began throwing the potatoes over the fence. Throwing them as far as we could. We just wanted to put as much distance between ourselves and the hot potatoes as we could.

About half the loot had been successfully launched over the nearest fence when my mother suddenly appeared at the back door.

'Come in here at once, both of you. There's someone at the door who is very keen to have a word with you.'

We looked at each other, looked down at the billycart and immediately dropped the potatoes we were holding. We had been caught in the act of disposing of the evidence. It was obviously time to face the not-so-sweet music.

Mr Porter, a tall, thin, man with a ruddy weather-beaten face, stood in the doorway blocking out the sunlight. The air around us was heavy with impending doom.

As it turned out, Mr Porter was quite forgiving. His manner was gruff, but not unreasonable given the situation. He had been able to track the potato-nappers because of a trail of tiny potatoes we had left as we journeyed home. We had succeeded where Hansel and Gretel had failed.

Mr Porter asked for an assurance that we would never steal his potatoes again, and we stood before him, shaking our heads in all the right places. He also asked for his potatoes back. It was at this point we wished we could immediately make ourselves invisible, or at the very least turn back time. We exchanged knowing glances, and my mum assured Mr Porter that his wishes would be met.

We dragged our tails from the scene and retired to the backyard to think of a solution. At this point, both of us managed to recover the ability to draw breath. We sat at the base of the washing line, surrounded by the family washing, pondering our fate as criminals.

Pondering on this problem didn't last long. Our fate was sealed by the untimely arrival of Mrs Dodd at the front door. Mrs Dodd lived two doors up from our house. She appeared most anxious. It was turning out to be a bad day for visitors.

A tiny, energetic woman with the harsh, raspy voice of a smoker, she appeared quite agitated when Mum opened the door. She had arrived with a strong sense of urgency about a minute after the disgruntled Mr Porter. She spluttered and coughed as she told a story about potatoes raining down on her backyard. Her voice became shriller as she told my mother, 'I thought I was going to get bopped on the noggin, and my poor cat – well she fled under the house like she'd been shot from a cannon!'

And so, we copped it for a second time in the same day. Robert was sent home in disgrace. I got the 'Wait till your father hears about this, he'll be mortified' routine and spent some more time in my room.

Dishes

Poetry exists in small moments too. It employs the use of powerful words in tight spaces. The simple act of doing the dishes can inspire words. My notebooks are littered with raw poetic pieces. I love the playfulness of poetry. Wordplay is at its peak when poetry is in the room. I trapped these words one evening after the washing-up team of my wife and me had effortlessly completed the task.

> We share the kitchen
> Washing the dishes
> There are too few to matter
> When it's tea for two
> We work instinctively
> Easily
> Back and forth
> At our respective tasks
> Washing, wiping
> Putting away
> Restoring order
> Never colliding
> Never bumping
> We glide
> Through our kitchen sink manoeuvres
> Each plate, fork, cup returns to its assigned place
> Conversation floats easily like background music
> Drifting through
> A moment
> A memory
> We measure the day
> The chore dissolves in a word sea
> We complete the task
> Rinse and wring
> Wipe and fold
> Unconsciously

> The dishes are done
> No Problem.
>
> *Alan j Wright*

Chicken Bones and Dead Umbrellas Walking on Union Street

A winter's day walk through Brooklyn's Park Slope inspired this little piece of poetry.

> On a wet, wild, windswept day
> The sidewalk –
> Shiny and slippery
> The last of the golden fall leaves
> Are plastered to the sidewalk
> A squelchy carpet
> For me to trudge over
> In my sturdy leather boots
> Amid the leaves I spot chicken bones
> And a dead umbrella.
>
> *Alan j Wright*

Backyard Blues

I was listening to Harry Manx's special brand of blues one day and this is what emerged, courtesy of my inner child. The blues are a familiar part of the human condition.

> Standing in the backyard
> Grumpy to the bone
> Slumped against the glum tree
> Miserable, alone
> Got those misery makin'
> Real heart breakin'
> Laughter takin'

Low down
Backyard blues
I've been grounded
Compounded
My friends are out runnin'
Funnin'
While I'm slumped against the glum tree
Grumpy to the bone
Got those sad makin'
Smile shakin'
Low down
Backyard blues
I'm dejected
Suspected
Terminally affected
Totally disconnected
Still slumped against the glum tree
With those no bike ridin'
Five day no play
Low down
Backyard blues.

Alan j Wright

Delving into Twelve

A mandatory visit to the supermarket inspired this notebook entry. It leaped into my conscious mind as I stood in the '12 items or less' queue. My frustration resulted in a notebook entry that was partly a persuasive piece and partly an unashamed rant!

> What is it about the number 12 that causes people such difficulty? Twelve is a most intriguing number. Most calendar systems have 12 months in a year. The Western zodiac has 12 signs, as does the Chinese zodiac. There are 24 hours in a day, with 12 hours in half a day. A new day starts with the midnight stroke.

Furthermore, the basic units of time (60 seconds, 60 minutes, 24 hours) are all perfectly divisible by twelve. Twelve squared is 144, also known as a gross. Twelve is a great number! Not gross in the slightest.

The concept of a dozen, however, seems to elude many of my fellow citizens, it seems. I was standing in the supermarket line patiently awaiting my turn at the checkout, and it became obvious that the customers in front of me had blatantly exceeded the '12 items or less' message, despite the fact that it was so clearly displayed for all to read.

Not a big deal? Well, the first few times it happened I let it roll by. Then I started silently counting just to confirm my suspicions. I ruminated on this a little more – maybe they figured if two of them strolled up to the checkout they were entitled to present at least 24 items. But I then noticed one person did all the handling of the items while the other stood silently by like a potted plant making no discernible contribution to the entire process. Others, I figured, had decided that seven tins of cat food registered as one item – cat food!

Mostly, though, I figured they didn't really give a flying fig what anybody else thought. For them, it was just a matter of convenience, and it sure beat standing in line behind a shopping trolley laden with enough produce to get a family of four through the winter, let alone a normal week.

Normally, I wait in the queue, gathering ideas about characters and dialogue or merely observing human interactions: kids grabbing at sweet temptations strategically placed within grasping distance, disaffected teens thumbing through trashy magazines as they wait, harassed mothers trying to will their errant toddlers through the stainless-steel corral, or tired robotic workers shuffling home with a few last-minute items.

As I stand in line, my mind has turned perversely to solutions to this problem of presenting more than 12 items. Maybe an alarm could ring when the magic number is exceeded, and the shameful shopper would then stand in the lonely square for five minutes while others tut-tutted as they hurried by. Maybe their excess items could be donated to charity. Maybe they could be slapped with a 12-day ban. Oh, the possibilities!

As you may infer, I am not good at supermarket shopping. I am a most reluctant hunter and gatherer. It is an act of last resort. I think I need to unwind, forget about the number 12, savour a coffee and enjoy a good read.

Birdsong Symphony

Writing ideas emerge when we listen. In this piece, the beauty of birdsong not only provided a glorious start to my day but also delivered a perfect reason to write.

> I woke early this morning. I woke in the twilight zone – that brief period of half light just before sunrise. Outside the bedroom window, a chorus of pre-dawn birdsong drew my immediate attention. A cacophony of noise, sounding like an orchestra in warm-up phase, grew in intensity as I slowly emerged from a state of sleep.
>
> Fully awake, I marvelled at the intensity of the chirruping. I was mesmerised by the massed voices of the winged warblers, their voices merging and colliding in the morning air as they strove to out-sing one another.
>
> After a time, the volume subsided somewhat, and identifiable voices emerged. The lilting song of the thrush contrasted with the sharp, shrill song of the parrots, the joyful cackle of the kookaburras and the soft, low cooing of the doves.
>
> The volume softened further until it was merely a twitter, before the carolling of the magpies rose up. What a glorious and somehow fitting finale they provided. This symphony of the morning had heralded the dawn of a new day, and as I lay

there in my bed, relishing those precious minutes before I hit the ground running, I reflected on how fortunate I had been to hear it. Small moments and simple pleasures are there to be savoured.

The Long-Awaited Visitors

On occasions, the writer finds himself or herself in the right place at the right time. After a wait of many years, my long-anticipated visitors finally arrived, and I was there to greet them.

> Today some special visitors came to my home. They quite literally flew in. I was sitting on the deck sharing a cup of tea in the faint autumn sunlight with my wife and a friend when I noticed some unexpected visitors hovering near the buddleias beside the creek.
>
> At first, I wasn't sure if I was seeing things. Such visits are uncommon. However, these particular visitors are renowned for being able to travel significant distances, and I have waited many years for them to grace me with their presence. So the hope in my heart began to dance with anticipation.
>
> I stood to obtain a closer look. I approached tentatively, not wishing to create a disturbance, still unsure if what my eyes were fixed upon matched the thoughts in my head. Were these magnificent butterflies that flittered around me actually the legendary monarch butterflies also known as wanderers? Diving and swooping continually around the buddleias and along the creek, their movement held me mesmerised. Finally, they flew up high and disappeared into the branches of a weeping willow before returning to the buddleias (butterfly bush) once more. They halted here momentarily to allow their delicate wings to soak up the vital sun. Their wings were like solar panels.
>
> Here they were resting on the buddleias that I had planted some three years before in the hope of attracting exotic butterflies, and now a cluster of what I strongly believed were the long-awaited

wanderers were feasting on the dark purple flowers of my black buddleias. This was the pay-off. This was the realisation of a simple dream. For years I had planted swan plants in the hope of attracting wanderers. It had been fruitless. Instead, they had found the buddleias.

I raced inside to grab my camera. I needed evidence. This took quite some time. The butterflies rarely settled long enough for me to get an all-important close-up. After some considerable time, I had some shots of my winged visitors.

I checked the photos I had taken against the photos of the monarch butterfly (wanderer) on the internet. They certainly looked the same. I then emailed my photos to my friend Barry, a butterfly aficionado. He confirmed my suspicions. 'They're wanderers all right.'

When you've waited so long for something to arrive, it's like being a kid again. You are alive with the thought and the moment. The wait for the wanderers was over!

CONSIDER

To invoke the famous words of the original television series *Mission Impossible*:

> 'Your mission, should you wish to accept it', is to launch and maintain your own writer's notebook. Fill it with your own slices of life, your own observation and pondering on the world, your very own personal writing projects. Maybe something you have read in this chapter may spark an idea for your own writing piece. May you find your inspiration easily.

18

FINAL REFLECTIONS

I find myself frequently pondering this writing life. Questions often arise surrounding the mystery of routines and rituals and what sparks one's passion for writing. Teachers and students are ever keen to engage in these types of conversations. Curiosity is abundant in such situations and often causes me to reflect upon my personal journey. Documenting some of the thoughts and experiences surrounding my writing life, I merely sat down with my notebook and unfolded the map of my writing life.

One of the earliest writing memories I recall was in Grade 3. I wrote a poem about 'Spring'. Back then we had little choice, The teacher chose the topic and the genre, and we were expected to respond. My little poem gained the favourable attention of a couple of my classmates, and they suggested I share it with our teacher, Mr Manzie. He was also suitably impressed and invited me to read it aloud to the entire class. I duly read it out, and they responded with clapping. I had never had this type of response to my written words. The exact wording of that early foray into poetry has long faded, but I have never forgotten how the experience made me feel. When we feel good about something we have produced, it delivers energy. We want more of that sense of accomplishment and we are encouraged to keep striving. I was hooked on poetry from that day. That moment.

I regret not having many pieces from those early writing days. We just weren't encouraged to value our writing in the way we now ask our students to do. The emphasis was firmly on what to write, not how to write. Students back then had no sense of agency around the writing they undertook. There was no encouragement to think metacognitively about your writing experiences. It was about getting the product completed. It was about teacher pleasing.

In high school I wrote numerous pieces for the school magazine, and when I entered college, I became editor of and contributor to the newspaper. My journey continued, and the connection grew increasingly stronger.

I am an eclectic writer. I write across a range of genres: plays, poetry, narratives, professional exposition and opinion pieces. I write across a range of media. I have willingly embraced social media as an outlet for sharing ideas.

As I stated at the beginning of this book, I started my first writer's notebook in 1983 and have been filling them with entries, ideas and observations ever since. Each notebook reveals a new part of my life's journey. My notebooks continue to evolve as I go, shape and size constantly changing to suit my preference at any particular time. I frequently share my notebooks with the students and teachers I work with across the many schools I visit. I view these notebooks as a key resource in my role as a teacher of writing. I am acutely aware of the responsibility I carry, modelling my role as writer, collector, experimenter and risk taker. I strive to show I am a brave writer.

I love words! Their sound, shape and application intrigue me. I write with my ear, frequently collecting quotes and random utterances I overhear. I am an eavesdropper, and proud of the fact. I find conversation fascinating. Words stick to my conscious mind along with facts and assorted trivia. I have my dad to thank for this. He celebrated words and shared this fascination with me from an early age. He raised my awareness of the power words convey, frequently engaging me in wordplay throughout my formative years. This immersion in etymology fostered my love of language, without doubt. I am a gongoozler. I love to observe things for periods of time. My eye is drawn also to glimpsing things. My mind attempts to journal the observations I make, be they close up or from a distance.

As mentioned previously, I have a well-developed obsession for black gel pens. I buy them in bulk. When I write with these magical pens, they assist me to believe (quite falsely, I might add) that I am a writer in possession of a really rapid writing hand. The words spread speedily across the pages of my notebooks, covering the white glare of the empty page in next to no time. In reality, I am left-handed and not all that quick. I am neat and organised, however, so it's not so bad, I figure. However, thanks to my special pen of choice, I experience a harmless delusion. Glide pen, glide…

I'll stop there. There's more to share, of course, but I'll reserve that for another time. I rapidly filled five pages in my notebook reflecting on my writing life and its influences. I'm certain there is more to emerge. I just have to dive back in the deep end and do some more exploration. I encourage my fellow writers of all ages to try it. What has shaped and continues to shape your writing life?

The Pursuit of Passions

As a child, I had an unquenchable passion for sport. Football, cricket and athletics were my three passions. Little else mattered. I devoted innumerable hours to perfecting my skills in these sporting zones. It was always football in winter, cricket and athletics in summer. The backyard of our house was the setting for my initial efforts, sometimes with friends and sometimes on my own. I kicked the football, leaped in the air and marked the ball, chased it, bounced it – round and round and round the yard. The football and I were almost constantly connected. The onset of darkness at the end of the day marked the end of my pursuit of my sporting dreams. They burned brightly. Things reached a point when my mother intervened and suggested I move my practice to a more appropriate setting because her flowers were constantly under attack from stray footballs. I was decimating her dahlias. Deadheading her roses. Smashing her sweet peas.

Cricket was much the same. Bat and ball were equally attended to as I lived out my passion for the summer game. Athletics allowed me to spend time running, jumping, leaping and throwing to my heart's content. In fact, my entire boyhood could be viewed as a scene of constant motion.

I held strongly to a vision of playing sport at the elite level from a very early age. I was a boy in a bubble of sporting fantasy. Emulating heroes and performing feats of sporting immortality were happening right there in my head – in our backyard or anywhere else I was in proximity to a ball. Pretty normal boy stuff really. In time, my dream fell short of that fame-filled sporting future, but the passion for sport has persisted to this day.

Another passion lay submerged within me at that time. It was a slow-burning passion, and it waited patiently for me to notice it. It made itself irresistible around the age of 11, when my Grade 6 teacher, Frank Harris, shared his particular passion for poetry and reading. *The Adventures of Tom Sawyer*, and the stories and poetry of Henry Lawson and Andrew Barton 'Banjo' Patterson, found a lasting place in my heart. The flames were thus fanned. Experiences like this helped me to recognise a passion. A passion that, for me, could sit quite comfortably alongside my sporting passion – a passion for literature. Fortunately I realised that such passions were not mutually exclusive. It's okay to like football and poetry at the same time!

I share these thoughts because I frequently encounter young learners in schools who see passion as a singular choice: sport or the arts, but not both. The culture in which they live frequently gives them such messages.

Who decides what your passions will be? Who has the right to tell an adolescent they can't gain equal delight from poetry and basketball, painting and football, cricket and music, ballet and screenwriting. Hopefully a more rounded adult emerges from such diverse pursuits. I follow my football team with an unbridled passion, just as I pursue my enduring passion for writing poetry. Why should anyone be denied the right to pursue more than one passion? The answer probably lies in societal pressures and some misguided view of what is acceptable. Such attitudes are often macho driven and frankly quite limiting.

The reality is that, as we age, our bodies tell us that while the passion for sport remains, the ability to actively participate slips away – like oil held in the hand. What remains are memories of past deeds and the effects of the accumulated injuries. I'm grateful that reading and writing are not contact sports. They are passions in which I can actively participate for the duration of my life. They are passions that can easily go the journey. That suits me fine.

Passion may be described in various ways; however, in this context I view passion as an intense inner drive. It embodies a feeling of commitment or strong devotion to some activity, object or concept. My particular passion for reading and writing sustains and comforts me. I am so grateful for this part of who I have become. May you, dear reader, readily find your passion or passions too.

My writer's notebook is a place to be honest, to write down what a writer needs to preserve and note. It is a place free of critics. My notebook is a place where I frequently discover I had more to say on a particular subject or issue than I originally believed.

My notebook contains the truth of my life – at least a version of it – and in that truth I am able to discover some of the treasure all our lives possess. I am a treasure hunter. Interestingly, none of us have any way of knowing whether what we find by way of words will prove important to someone else at some later stage. We cannot know if they will understand. If a reader appreciates my gathered words, that's a bonus.

My notebook is a place to practise risk taking. It is where I can indulge in some experimentation with words and ideas. The very act of writing stimulates my creativity. The pieces that grow within the covers of this book are invaluable to me as a writer, for they are the foundation of the longer pieces that later emerge as I move up and out of the notebook into other phases of my writing. The entries gathered across several notebooks formed the basis of my previous book on writing: *Igniting Writing: When a Teacher Writes* (Wright, 2011). The words were stored within, awaiting my return.

It's for me that I write, and initially it's for me to try to understand what prompted my thoughts and ideas. I am writing to save my life. My time. My truth. If I don't write, my tiny place in history slowly evaporates. My notebook life has increased my awareness of my world. So, as much as the time I spend lost in my notebook takes me away, it has hopefully strengthened my connections to others, with the insights this time has provided. My notebook is like a garden. If I continue to feed it, things will flourish. My notebook writing life has taught me these things, and that's the truth.

It is at this point that the word 'next' looms into view. The word 'next' is super important to teacher and student writers alike.

What will you write about next?

What are you going to read next?

What will you explore next?

Where will you write next?

BIBLIOGRAPHY

Atwell, Nancie. (1987). *In the Middle: Writing, Reading, and Learning with Adolescents.* Heinemann Educational Books.

Badami, S. (2015). In your dreams. In D. Adelaide (Ed.), *The Simple Act of Reading.* Vintage Books.

Bansch, Helga. (2011). *Odd Bird Out.* Gecko Press.

Berger, Thomas. (n.d.) [Quotation]. Goodreads. https://www.goodreads.com/quotes/14477-why-do-writers-write-because-it-isn-t-there

Bird, Carmel. (1988). *Dear Writer.* McPhee Gribble.

Blake, Quentin. (2008). Writers' rooms. *Guardian.* https://www.theguardian.com/books/2008/may/23/writers.rooms.roald.dahl

Bradbury, Ray. (2015). *Zen in the Art of Writing.* Voyager GB.

Brophy, J. (2008). Developing students' appreciation for what is taught in school. *Educational Psychologist, 43*(3), 132–41.

Buckner, Aimee. (2005). *Notebook Knowhow.* Stenhouse.

Dillard, Annie. (1974). *Pilgrim at Tinker Creek.* Harper's Magazine Press.

Dillard, Annie. (1990). *The Writing Life.* Harper and Row.

Doyle, Roddy. (2014). *Brilliant.* Macmillan Children's Books.

Ehrlich, Amy (Ed.). (1996). *When I Was Your Age: Original Stories about Growing Up.* Candlewick.

Fletcher, A. (2016). Exceeding expectations: Scaffolding agentic engagement through assessment as learning. *Educational Research, 58*(4), 400–19.

Fletcher, Ralph. (1992). *What a Writer Needs.* Heinemann.

Fletcher, Ralph. (1996a). *Breathing In, Breathing Out: Keeping A Writer's Notebook.* Heinemann.

Fletcher, Ralph. (1996b). *A Writer's Notebook: Unlocking the Writer within You.* Avon Books.

Fletcher, Ralph. (2010). *Pyrotechnics on the Page: Playful Craft That Sparks Writing.* Stenhouse.

Garrett, L., & Moltzen, R. (2011). Writing because I want to, not because I have to. *English Teaching: Practice and Critique, 10*(1), 165–80.

Gleitzman, Morris. (2001). *Adults Only*. Penguin Books.
Graves, Donald. (1983). *Writing: Teachers and Children at Work*. Heinemann.
Griffiths, Andy. (2013). *Once Upon A Slime: 45 Ways to get writing… Fast!* Pan McMillan.
Hemingway, Ernest. (1964). *A Moveable Feast*. Jonathan Cape.
Herrick, Steven. (2016). *Another Night in Mullet Town*. University of Queensland Press.
Johnston, Peter H. (2004). *Choice Words: How Our Language Affects Children's Learning*. Routledge.
Kellogg, Ronald T. (1994). *The Psychology of Writing*. Oxford University Press.
Kleon, Austin. (2024). The notebook is where you figure out what's going on [Blog]. https://austinkleon.com/2024/09/07/the-notebook-is-where-you-figure-out-whats-going-on/
Levine, Mel. (2003). *The Myth of Laziness*. Simon and Schuster.
Lunn, Hugh. (2006). *Lost for Words: Australia's Lost Language in Words and Stories*. Australian Broadcasting Commission Books.
Macfarlane, Robert. (2015). *Landmarks*. Penguin.
Nye, Naomi Shihab. (1996). Thoughts about notebooks.
Plimpton, George. (1958). Ernest Hemmingway: The Art of Fiction [Interview]. *Paris Review 21*.
Powling, Chris. (1985) *Roald Dahl: A Fascinating Profile of a Master Storyteller*. Puffin.
Prine, John. (1971). *Angel from Montgomery* [Music & lyrics].
Rolls, Eric. (1986). *Celebration of the Senses*. Penguin.
Rylant, Cynthia. (1995). *The Van Gogh Café*. Harcourt Brace.
Schneider, Pat. (2005). *Writing Alone and with Others*. Oxford University Press.
Smith, Keri. (2008). *How to Be an Explorer of the World*. Penguin.
Spinelli, Jerry. (1990). *Maniac Magee*. Little, Brown.
Thiele, Colin. (1974). *The Rim of the Morning: Six Stories*. Seal Books.
Thomas, Lewis. (1983). Seven wonders. *New York Times*.
Thoreau, Henry D. (1962). *The Journal of Henry D. Thoreau*. Dover Publications.
Winton, Tim. (2015). *Island Home: A Landscape Memoir*. Hamish Hamilton.
Wood Ray, Katie. (2006). *Study Driven*. Heinemann.
Woodson, Jacqueline. (2014). *Brown Girl Dreaming*. Penguin.
Wright, Alan, J. (2011) *Igniting Writing: When a Teacher Writes*. Hawker Brownlow Education.
Wright, Alan J. (2014). *Searching for Hen's Teeth: Poetry from the Search Zone*. Balboa Press.
Wright, Alan, J. (2016). *I Bet There's No Broccoli on the Moon: More Poetry from the Search Zone*. Balboa Press.
Young, Ross & Ferguson, Felicity. (2020). *Real-World Writers: A Handbook for Teaching Writing with 7–11 Year Olds*. Taylor & Francis.
Zolotow, Charlotte. (2017). *The Seashore Book*. Charlesbridge Children.

ABOUT THE AUTHOR

Alan j Wright is an Australian education consultant, writer and poet whose enduring career has been guided by his belief in empowering learners to become independent and self-directed. A curious learner himself, Alan has striven to model and behave as a living, breathing advocate for living a literate life. Over five decades, he has worked as a teacher, principal and consultant to promote choice and voice in literacy education. Across that time, he has maintained a profile as a teacher who writes, remaining committed to the belief that literacy is an empowering force that every child deserves to access. He has worked with schools and school systems throughout Australia and internationally to promote the effective teaching of literacy.

www.ingramcontent.com/pod-product-compliance
Lightning Source LLC
Chambersburg PA
CBHW052027070526
44584CB00016B/1939